Photo by Godfrey Argent

GUILD LIBRARY

"MOVE OVER, MRS. MARKHAM"

A Comedy

by

Ray Cooney and John Chapman

ENGLISH THEATRE GUILD LTD
Ascot House, 52 Dean Street, London W1V 6BJ

"MOVE OVER MRS. MARKHAM" was presented by Peter Saunders in association with Ray Cooney on March 17th 1971, at the Vaudeville Theatre, London, with the following cast:

JOANNA MARKHAM	Moira Lister
ALISTAIR SPENLOW	Trevor Bannister
SYLVIE	Susan Edmonstone
LINDA LODGE	Lana Morris
PHILIP MARKHAM	Tony Britton
HENRY LODGE	Terence Alexander
WALTER PANGBOURNE	Bryan Coleman
OLIVE HARRIET SMYTHE	Cicely Courtneidge
MISS WILKINSON	Ann Kennedey

Directed by RAY COONEY

The first production of this play was at the Richmond Theatre on July 21st, 1969. It subsequently played the Palace Theatre, Westcliff, with the following cast:

JOANNA MARKHAM	Virginia Stride
ALISTAIR SPENLOW	Simon Brent
SYLVIE	Sandra Fehr
LINDA LODGE	Angela Browne
PHILIP MARKHAM	Ray Cooney
HENRY LODGE	William Franklyn
WALTER PANGBOURNE	John Clegg
MISS SMYTHE	Carole Allen
MISS WILKINSON	Caroline Seymour

SOME PRESS APPRECIATION

"A riot. The laughter hit of the year ... I never stopped laughing"

—John de Pre. The People

"Filled the Vaudeville with rapturously demonstrative joy."
—Harold Hobson. Sunday Times

"Naughty nonsense at its greatest"
—Herbert Kretzmer. Daily Express

"Writers Ray Cooney and John Chapman at the peak of their craft."

—Peter Lewis. Daily Mail

"Very funny"   *John Barber. Daily Telegraph*

"The dialogue is risque and amusing and the acting splendid, matching the lightning pace of Ray Cooney's direction ... it should run for years."   *Clive Hirschhorn. Sunday Express*

"Reaches splendid heights of lunacy."
—Michael Billington. The Times

"Will delight the Town for a very long time."
—Milton Shulman. Evening Standard

"Very funny, highly expert."   *—Felix Barker. Evening News*

"You're a riot Mrs. M. ... A slick, frantic riot of an evening ... a wildly funny explosion."   *David Gillard. Daily Sketch*

". . . So funny is this that it hurts." *—Jeremy Kingston. Punch*

Cast in order of appearance

JOANNA MARKHAM
ALISTAIR SPENLOW
SYLVIE
LINDA LODGE
PHILIP MARKHAM
HENRY LODGE
WALTER PANGBOURNE
OLIVE HARRIET SMYTHE
MISS WILKINSON

The action of the play takes place in Mr. and Mrs. Markham's top floor London flat on a summer evening.

ACT 1. About 7.00 p.m.

INTERVAL

ACT 2. The same. The action is continuous.

ACT ONE

The action of the play takes place in a very elegant top floor London flat. A composite set of drawing room and bedroom is divided roughly into two-thirds and one-third respectively. The bedroom is stage L. and the wall between the two rooms is suggested by a practical door set upstage at right angle to the setting line. The flat has just been decorated in an arresting though tasteful style. In the bedroom there is an oval bed, over which protrudes from the wall L. on a bracket, a lamp. There is also a dressing table L. with telephone, a door off L. to the dressing room and a recessed window in the back wall through which can be seen the skyline of London. The drawing room has an archway U.R. leading into a hallway which goes off right one way and off left the other way. Off left leads to front door and kitchen. Off right goes to the au pair's room. Between the archway and the bedroom are two doors. The one nearer the bedroom leads into a study. To the right of the study is a sliding door into an opulent drinks dispensary. All the doors on the set except the study door are louvred. In the wall R. is a long window. The important furniture is a sofa down right centre of the drawing room, an armchair down left centre, a low pouffe down left and a small coffee table in front of the sofa. There is a small desk below the window right on which is an intercom telephone with a buzzer and an ordinary telephone. Time: about 7 p.m. on a warm summer evening.

The CURTAIN RISES on an empty stage. After a moment we hear JOANNA MARKHAM calling out:

JOANNA (off). Philip—Darling, I'm back.

(She enters from HALLWAY. She is an attractive and sophisticated woman in her thirties. She is carrying a few parcels from some of London's exclusive stores and her handbag, which she puts on the desk R. She appears to be in a hurry and is attempting to remove her hat and gloves as she dumps most of her parcels on the sofa. She opens the bedroom door and calls):

1

JOANNA (cont). Philip!
(She goes on into the dressing room)

JOANNA (as she goes). Are you home, dear?

(ALISTAIR SPENLOW appears from the study. He is in his twenties, good-looking and London's latest fashionable interior designer. Underneath his slightly arty exterior lurks a virile male. He enters carrying curtain material which is draped round him like a toga and a tape measure round his neck.)

ALISTAIR. Mrs. Markham—is that you, Mrs. Markham?
JOANNA (calls). Who's that?
ALISTAIR (calls). Mr. Spenlow (To himself) I feel more like bloody Nero.

(JOANNA re-enters from the dressing room.)

JOANNA. Oh, you're working late, Alistair.
ALISTAIR (indicating). I'm trying to finalise your husband's study there.
JOANNA. I expect he's still downstairs in the office.
ALISTAIR. Well, I'm having a tiny fit up here, darling.
JOANNA (patting him casually on the cheek). I'm sure it'll look super. Now be a dear sweet boy and pour us both a drink.

(She moves to the intercom telephone.)

ALISTAIR. I haven't time for drinks, Mrs. Markham.

(JOANNA presses the button on the intercom.)

ALISTAIR (cont.) It's very difficult when he doesn't give me a yay or nay on anything.
JOANNA. Have a cup of coffee.
ALISTAIR. I don't want a cup of coffee. I want a decision.
JOANNA (into phone). Philip dear, are you coming up? . . . Don't forget we're dining out tonight. . . . Well, ask Henry not to keep you too long down there.
ALISTAIR (whispering). Ask him about the curtains. (Showing her the material.)
JOANNA (into phone). Oh—Mr. Spenlow's started work on your study and wants to give you peacock blue curtains.

ALISTAIR. And tomato chair covers.

JOANNA (into phone). And tomato chair covers . . . I see.

(She replaces the phone)

ALISTAIR. How does he feel about that?

JOANNA. Rather strongly.

ALISTAIR. Oh really! (He throws the tape meausure on the desk.) I've never known a job drag on as long as your flat. I could have tarted up the Albert Hall in this time.

JOANNA. I know you've met with a little opposition from Mr. Markham—

ALISTAIR. Little! I hate to say it, but your husband is as unsophisticated as those children's books he publishes.

JOANNA. You might possibly say his taste was old-fashioned.

ALISTAIR. If he'd had his way with his "cream paint, chintz and mahogany furniture," it would have finished up like Peter Rabbit's parlour.

JOANNA. He's been jolly sweet and given in on most things.

ALISTAIR. Took me three weeks to talk him into a floral bidet. And I'll tell you another thing, if he and his partner want anything done to their suite of offices on the ground floor I'll give them a bucket of off-white, half a dozen beige curtains and a "do-it-yourself" kit.

JOANNA. Now, now, no temperaments, please. (Calls out.) Sylvie!

SYLVIE (off). Yes, Mrs. Markham?

JOANNA. Sylvie, will you get a coffee for Mr. Spenlow, please. (To ALISTAIR.) You'll feel better after that.

ALISTAIR. God, one more coffee here and my liver will start percolating.

(SYLVIE HAUSER, the Swiss au pair girl, enters. She is a gorgeous big blonde who speaks English with hardly any accent)

SYLVIE. What was that, Mrs Markham?

JOANNA. Would you very kindly get a coffee for Mr. Spenlow.

SYLVIE. Certainly.

ALISTAIR. Well, a small one.

JOANNA. And I'd like a gin and French.

SYLVIE. Certainly.

JOANNA. A large one. And then you can go. It's your night off, isn't it?

SYLVIE. Yes.

JOANNA. And don't look so miserable, Alistair, it may never happen.

ALISTAIR. No, I don't think it will.

(JOANNA moves towards the bedroom.)

SYLVIE (referring to the parcels). You've been shopping, Mrs. Markham?

JOANNA. Yes, I couldn't make up my mind what to wear for this "do" tonight so I bought two new dresses.

SYLVIE. And have you decided which one to wear?

JOANNA (innocently). My old black one I think.

(She exits into dressing room.)

SYLVIE. Would you like anything with your coffee, Mr. Spenlow?

ALISTAIR. I certainly would.

(He throws down the material then takes her in his arms and gives her a passionate kiss.)

SYLVIE (coming out of the kiss). Anything else?

ALISTAIR. (lustily). God, you're sexy. (He kisses her again.)

SYLVIE. No, no, darling. Mr. Markham may be coming upstairs from his office in a minute.

ALISTAIR. He wouldn't know the difference between a sexy kiss and a salt beef sandwich.

(He goes to kiss her again)

SYLVIE. No, no, be patient.

ALISTAIR. I've been patient for weeks.

SYLVIE. Well, they're both out tonight, we will have the place to ourselves.

ALISTAIR. Marvellous.

(He bends down to pick up his material and SYLVIE gooses his bottom. He straightens up quickly.)

ALISTAIR (cont). I wish I'd never taught you that.
SYLVIE. I do the goose quite well, yes?
ALISTAIR. You do the goose very well, yes.

(JOANNA enters from dressing room and calls out.)

JOANNA (entering). How's my drink coming along?
SYLVIE. I'm sorry, I was delayed.

(She gives ALISTAIR a very quick kiss just before JOANNA comes through.)

JOANNA. Don't worry, I'll see to it. You go and get Mr. Spenlow's coffee, would you?

(She goes into the drinks bar.)

ALISTAIR (innocently). You know how I like it?
SYLVIE (with a wink). Not yet, Mr. Spenlow.

(As she starts to go, ALISTAIR gives her a goose.)

SYLVIE (cont). Oops!
JOANNA (looking out). What?
ALISTAIR (innocently). Nothing.

(The front door bell rings. It is a very fanciful chime which goes on for some time.)

SYLVIE. I'll get it, Mrs. Markham.

(She exits.)

ALISTAIR (enthusiastically referring to bell). Listen!

(He and JOANNA listen to the bell until it finally stops.)

JOANNA. Perhas we ought to reconsider the front door bell.
ALISTAIR. It's unique!

JOANNA. Yes. I think the third movement drags a little.

(LINDA LODGE enters. She is a woman in her thirties, very vivacious but slightly scatter-brained.)

LINDA. Darling. Darling, disaster!

JOANNA. What on earth's the matter, Linda?

LINDA. Absolute disaster.

ALISTAIR. Hullo, Mrs. Lodge.

LINDA. Would you mind, Mr. Spenlow.

ALISTAIR. Not at all. How do you think it's all looking?

LINDA. Divine.

ALISTAIR. Now be honest, Mrs. Lodge. What do you think about the front door bell?

LINDA. What front door bell.

ALISTAIR. Oh, ding bloody dong. (He exits temperamentally into study.)

LINDA. Joanna, my sweet, are our darling husbands still downstairs in the office?

JOANNA. I think so. Philip should be up any minute now to change. We're going to that dreary publishers' dinner.

LINDA. Oh God. He'll probably bring Henry up for a quick drink. Give them a buzz on that intercom thing.

JOANNA (moving to desk). Don't tell me you've landed yourself in another crisis?

LINDA. To end all!

JOANNA (picks up the intercom phone). You haven't crashed the car again? (She buzzes through.)

LINDA. Yes, but that's got nothing to do with it. Find out how long they're going to be.

JOANNA (on phone). Oh, hullo, Henry—

LINDA (quickly whispers). Don't tell Henry I'm here!

JOANNA (to LINDA). Mm?

LINDA. Just see how long they're going to be.

JOANNA (on phone). No, no. It's all right. I don't want to speak to Philip. I just wondered when he might be coming up. ... Finishing what? (to LINDA.) They're still checking the proof copy of "Harry the Hornet".

LINDA. Good!

JOANNA (on phone). No. No hurry. Finish it. Oh, Henry, is that the one where Harry the Hornet falls in love with Winnie the Wasp?

LINDA (impatiently). Darling!

JOANNA (still engrossed on phone). What did the author finally decide about the ending . . . oh, I think it's a pity. . . . No, I don't believe three-year olds give a damn about the problems of mixed marriages. I thought if Winnie the Wasp had some children—

LINDA (whispering). Put the wretched thing down!

JOANNA (on phone). 'Bye, Henry. (Puts phone down.)

LINDA. Now, darling, listen. You won't be involved in the slightest.

JOANNA. Involved in what?

LINDA. And keep terribly calm because there's nothing to worry about.

JOANNA. I'm glad to hear it.

LINDA. We just want to borrow your flat for the evening.

JOANNA (puzzled). What?

LINDA. Just for this evening.

JOANNA. You and Henry?

LINDA. No, me and Walter.

JOANNA. Walter!?

LINDA. I've told you a little bit about Walter.

JOANNA. Have you?

LINDA. You know. Walter Pangbourne.

JOANNA. Oh yes. You met him at one of those evening classes you go to.

LINDA. That's it. "Tapestry for beginners".

JOANNA. I'd rather not hear any more.

LINDA. Oh, Joanna, don't be cross me with me. I've been a faithful wife for 14 years and a fat lot of good it's done me.

JOANNA. Well I suppose if you've fallen out of love with your husband—

LINDA. I haven't. I still adore him and so do his sectretaries, typists, receptionists. I've become a member of the Rotary Club. And it's no good giving me a conscience.

JOANNA. How about a gin and French.

LINDA. No I mustn't.

JOANNA. But you will.

LINDA. Of course.

(JOANNA goes into the bar but remains in view to the audience as she dispenses the drink.)

JOANNA. Honestly the strain of having a lover would give me ulcers.

LINDA. I'm hoping it'll cure mine.

JOANNA. But aren't you afraid Henry might find out?

LINDA. Henry? No, darling, he's much too busy trying to cover up his own tracks. Poor old Henry, it's always the same story it never varies "Sorry, darling—you know the publishing business another late night entertaining a client".

JOANNA. I'm sure half the gossip you hear about Henry isn't true.

LINDA. Not true? He must have more satisfied clients than the Prudential.

(By now they have their drinks.)

JOANNA. That's still no excuse for making whoopee with Walter.

LINDA. We haven't made anything yet, that's why we want to borrow the flat.

(ALISTAIR hurries in from study.)

ALISTAIR. Hang about, dears. Hang about. Is anyone sitting on my pinking shears?

JOANNA. I hope not.

ALISTAIR. Oh here they are.

LINDA. Now do go away, Mr. Spenlow. We're trying to have som ladies talk.

ALISTAIR. Super, give me a shout when it starts to hot up. (He exits study.)

LINDA. Now darling, can we borrow the flat?

JOANNA. It really is asking an awful lot.

LINDA. Why? You and Philip are out at this dinner and it's Sylvie's night off, isn't it?

JOANNA. That's all jolly fine, but what'll I say to Philip?

LINDA. Not a word, I hope, this is just between us, darling. When you get back you won't even know we've been here.

JOANNA. I wouldn't involve you in my affair.

LINDA. I didn't know you were having one!

JOANNA. I'm not. Philip and I couldn't carry on like that.

LINDA. It's always been my opinion that Philip doesn't carry on at all.

JOANNA. He certainly doesn't.

LINDA. Even with you.

JOANNA. What are you talking about?

LINDA. He's not exactly the demonstrative type, is he?

JOANNA. Of course he is—when he finds the time. While your Henry's out gallavanting every night poor old Philip's sitting up in bed reading children's books for the firm.

LINDA. All right, all right.

JOANNA. No wonder he doesn't feel amorous after forty-five minutes of Harry the Hornet. Anyway having had several satisfying years it's quite normal to ease up.

LINDA. Ease up, yes, but not fizzle out.

JOANNA. We have not fizzled out! Let's just stick to your problem.

LINDA. Oh my God yes. Well you see. We were going to spend tonight, our very first night at Walter's place.

(LINDA takes a 3 page letter from her handbag.)

JOANNA: So why don't you?

LINDA. Well, this afternoon I got this letter. You see, Walter's got a mother.

JOANNA. Has he. Poor soul.

LINDA. He'd arranged for her to go away for a few days.

JOANNA. What's gone wrong?

LINDA. The whole thing's fallen through. Poor Walter is beside himself.

JOANNA. I think that's the safest place for him.

LINDA. Darling, you've got to help us, you can see how desperate he is. (She hands JOANNA Page one.)

JOANNA (reading the opening). "My dear precious promise of paradise—" (glances at LINDA).

LINDA. I think that sums me up.

JOANNA. I think it sums Walter up. (Reading.) "The most devastating thing has happened. Mother's gone to bed with some little thing . . ." They're quite a family, aren't they?

LINDA. Walter's so disappointed, and he's been frightfully patient.

JOANNA. I'm sure.

LINDA. And it can't be good for him.

JOANNA. No. (Reading.) "I'll never forget the excitement I felt when you finally succumbed to my overtures. It was when we were having tea and cakes—on the roof garden at Derry and Toms. That wonderful afternoon—

LINDA (handing her a page). Page two.

JOANNA. . . . left me completely breathless. What more

can one say about moments like that. Sheer perfection. I know how difficult it is for you to get away with a husband etc. But please try to arrange something. I quite fancy the idea of trying—" (to LINDA, interested). Yes, yes? (LINDA hands her next page.) Oh. (Reads.) "your friend's place. Love and kisses, Walter." (JOANNA puts the pages of the letter on the sofa.) This is taking friendship too far.

LINDA. There'll be no problems. Walter and I will be here from, say, half past eight to ten thirty. That's two hours flat.

(JOANNA shoots her a look at the unintended double meaning.)

LINDA (cont.). Please.
JOANNA (weakening). Look I must get ready.

(JOANNA goes into the bedroom followed by LINDA who has picked up the pages of the letter from the sofa.)

LINDA. Just think of the happiness you'll be giving to Walter.
JOANNA. Why on earth can't you use a hotel? (She goes into the dressing room.)
LINDA. A hotel's too risky. We might bump into someone.

(She exits after JOANNA into the dressing room as PHILIP and HENRY enter. PHILIP is carrying several children's books. He is a pleasant looking man, studious, but with a worried air which comes from years of being on the losing side of life. HENRY, on the other hand, is successful, rakish and full of masculine confidence. He carries a slim briefcase.)

PHILIP. Henry, please.
HENRY. Come off it, Philip.
PHILIP. I've got enough on my plate with this damn decorator fellow—look at it—it's like living on a stand in the Ideal Home Exhibition.
HENRY. I gather Linda wants him to do our flat next.
PHILIP. You're welcome—have you seen the bedroom?
HENRY. No.
PHILIP. They've delivered the lamp post—just waiting for the bus stop. (He indicates the bedroom.)

(HENRY chuckles.)

HENRY. Talking of bedrooms what time are you clearing off tonight?

PHILIP. Henry, please. Look, I'm not happy about it.

HENRY. It's all settled, Philip.

PHILIP. I'm beginning to wish it wasn't.

HENRY. But, Philip, my dear old friend, you agreed. You can't go back on your word.

PHILIP. What I don't understand is why you and the—er—young lady can't go to a hotel.

HENRY. No. Hotels are always so damned impersonal, I prefer my *home* comforts.

PHILIP. *My* home comforts, you mean. I'm beginning to think the only reason you put me in this flat was for your own nefarious purposes.

HENRY. What a dreadful suggestion. I gave you this flat right over the office because as my partner I wanted you on the spot.

PHILIP. And that's just where you've got me.

HENRY. There's gratitude.

PHILIP. Doesn't it worry you, the number of women you get involved with?

HENRY. Yes. I used to have hundreds of 'em.

PHILIP. I think you behave pretty poorly. Especially for a man who publishes children's books.

HENRY. Are you suggesting an undertaker shouldn't go out with live people?

(PHILIP angrily moves to desk.)

HENRY (cont.). What I do in my private life has nothing to do with the business.

PHILIP. You're so busy with your private life we've hardly got any business.

(PHILIP sits at desk sorting out the children's books.)

HENRY. You do exaggerate.

PHILIP. Our firm hasn't published a best seller for years.

HENRY. You can talk. Who was the one who let the "Noddy" books slip through our fingers?

12

PHILIP. I thought you'd bring Noddy up again.

HENRY. Yes. Said you couldn't see any future for a little boy with a stiff neck and a bell on his head.

PHILIP. Don't change the subject, Henry. There is no excuse for your sort of behaviour.

HENRY. Who's excusing it? I just want to enjoy it.

PHILIP. You're emotionally immature.

HENRY. That's great coming from someone who's about as sexy as Mrs. Tiggywinkle. Anyway, I don't want any lectures now, just a little co-operation for tonight.

PHILIP. I find the whole thing so exhausting.

(He rises moving away.)

HENRY. All you're doing is going out to dinner. I'm the one who'll be exhausted.

PHILIP. I mean mentally. You only mentioned this girl-friend of yours yesterday afternoon and by 7.30 I'd come out in a nervous rash and had to go to bed.

HENRY. Proved very beneficial. You got through a book of nursery rhymes and two schoolgirls' annuals.

PHILIP. Look, I've got all the complications of having a mistress and you've got all the fun.

HENRY. Would you like me to fix you up with some nice, young—

PHILIP. No! The way you deceive your wife is appalling.

HENRY. Not to mention clever. The way I look at it I'm doing her a favour. It keeps me in good health, good spirits—

PHILIP. And pretty good practice.

HENRY. That's what I mean. Linda benefits as well.

PHILIP. I'm sure she must get suspicious about all your late nights.

HENRY. No. She's lost in admiration for my selfless attitude to the firm. Out nearly every evening entertaining our authors. Our authors would be staggered at the number of times they've been entertained.

PHILIP. And who is it "supposed" to be tonight?

HENRY. An elderly schoolmaster from Harrow.

PHILIP. Elderly schoolmaster?

HENRY. Who's written a gripping tale of an adventurous tortoise.

PHILIP. Good Lord.

HENRY. If you're going to tell a lie, tell a whopper.

PHILIP. And I suppose the "old fogey's" nineteen, blue-eyed and blonde.

HENRY. I've no idea what she looks like.

PHILIP. What?

HENRY. I've never met her. Only spoken to her. She's a telephone operator.

PHILIP. Oh, no.

HENRY. We got chatting and made a date for tonight.

PHILIP. Well I know the G.P.O. are trying to improve their service, but really.

HENRY. I was booking a personal call to the Continent, you know the French publisher we—

PHILIP. Yes, yes. What about this operator?

HENRY. Well I knew I was on to a good thing the way she said, "What time do you want it and where would you like me to get hold of you?"

(HENRY opens his briefcase and takes out his pyjama top.)

PHILIP. I still think you should have gone to a hotel. (Taking pyjamas.) Put those away.

(PHILIP goes to put them in the briefcase and stops.)

PHILIP (cont.). Where are the trousers?

HENRY. You sweet old-fashioned thing.

(PHILIP walks away in disgust. As HENRY puts the pyjamas back, ALISTAIR enters from the study with curtains and chair covers.)

ALISTAIR (as he enters). Mrs. Markham, would you please come—(sees PHILIP). Ah, you dear sweet man, you're back.

PHILIP. Oh Lord!

ALISTAIR. And a happy New Year to you too.

HENRY. He's busy, Spenlow.

ALISTAIR. I want him to come into the study and give a decision on these fabrics. I've already explained to Mrs. Markham that the tomato chair covers—

PHILIP. Whichever one you like.

ALISTAIR. It's your study, you must have a preference, ducky.

PHILIP. No, Mr. Spenlow, I have not. I wanted the flat to

be like our old house, plenty of polished mahogany—and cream paint.

ALISTAIR (with PHILIP). And cream paint.

PHILIP. Yes! It was my wife who decided to engage an interior decorator.

ALISTAIR. Designer.

PHILIP. What's the difference?

HENRY. The size of the bill.

ALISTAIR (grinning cheekily at HENRY). You wicked thing, you.

PHILIP (to ALISTAIR). Would you mind pressing on without me.

ALISTAIR. I only want a bijou fraction of your time.

PHILIP. That's what you always say, and you've been here for three months. (To HENRY.) It took him a fortnight to settle the au pair's room.

ALISTAIR. Yes, well of course I was rather delayed in there.

PHILIP. And from my point of view it was a complete waste of time.

ALISTAIR. And mine up till now. (Turns hastily to HENRY.) But, Mr. Lodge, he must surely admit the new bathroom's nothing short of an extravaganza.

HENRY. I'm sure he does.

PHILIP. Yes, I don't know how I ever existed without a floral bidet and a mauve low-level lavatory.

ALISTAIR. Well there you are. Now hurry up, I'm not going until I get a decision on the study.

HENRY. Oh aren't you. (Quickly pushes PHILIP towards the study.) Come on, let's give him one.

ALISTAIR. Thank you, Mr. Lodge. He wouldn't care if I hung half a dozen yards of tin foil—(to Henry) after you.

(HENRY exits to study.)

ALISTAIR (cont.). (Then baldly to PHILIP.) I'm sure you've got a better tie for that suit.

PHILIP. Yes I have. It's mahogany, with cream spots.

(He exits into study followed by ALISTAIR.)

ALISTAIR (as he exits). Cheeky.

(LINDA enters from the dressing room followed by JOANNA carrying the black dress she's going to wear, which she lays on the bed.)

LINDA. Thank you. You are a poppet, Joanna.
JOANNA. And you're a naughty girl, Linda.
LINDA. I'll do my best.

(They continue on into the sitting room.)

JOANNA. Now remember as far as I'm concerned, this is the only time.
LINDA. Don't worry. I won't ask anything more of you. Oh, you haven't got any champagne have you?
JOANNA. No. We haven't any oysters either.
LINDA. Well I must get some champagne, it's Walter's favourite thing. Well so far.

(LINDA moves to archway as SYLVIE enters with a cup of coffee on a tray.)

LINDA (cont.). Goodnight, Sylvie.
SYLVIE. Goodnight, Madam.

(LINDA exits.)

SYLVIE (cont.) Here is Mr. Spenlow's coffee.
JOANNA. Would you just take it into the study?
SYLVIE. Right.
JOANNA (suddenly). Oh, Sylvie. Tonight is your night off, isn't it?
SYLVIE. Yes.
JOANNA. Good, that's what I thought. And, Sylvie?
SYLVIE. Yes, Mrs. Markham?
JOANNA. You are definitely going to have it off?
SYLVIE. Oh yes, Mrs. Markham.

(PHILIP and ALISTAIR enter arguing, from the study.)

PHILIP. I'm sorry, Mr. Spenlow, but I just don't like anything about it.
ALISTAIR. That's a bit sweeping, you can't tell till it's finished.
PHILIP. I shan't feel any differently then. (Sees JOANNA.) Hello, dear.

JOANNA. Hello, sweetie. (She gives him a kiss.) Nothing wrong is there?

PHILIP. Nothing more than usual. Thank you, Sylvie, just what I need.

SYLVIE. No, this is for Mr. Spenlow.

PHILIP (piqued). I do beg his pardon.

ALISTAIR. He grants it. (Takes coffee.) Thanks, Sylvie.

(He gives her a surreptitious goose and she exits into hall. JOANNA puts her arm through PHILIP's.)

JOANNA. Have you been upsetting Alistair again?

PHILIP. Certainly not. He's been upsetting me. I can't see why we have to have someone else's ghastly taste foisted on to us.

ALISTAIR. Ghastly!?

JOANNA (to PHILIP). I promise you Alistair is really 'with it'.

PHILIP. Is he?

JOANNA. I mean look at his gorgeous clothes. I wish you'd have some made like that.

PHILIP. Me?

JOANNA (smiling). I'll pay for your corsets.

(ALISTAIR hoots with laughter. PHILIP glares at him and ALISTAIR's laugh fades.)

ALISTAIR (on his dignity). I'll just float back to the study. That's where I'll be if you want me.

PHILIP. I don't imagine we will.

ALISTAIR. Force yourself.

(ALISTAIR exits.)

PHILIP. I don't know how I've stood that chap all this time

JOANNA. You mustn't let him make you so edgy.

PHILIP (thinking of HENRY). Well it's not only *him*.

JOANNA. Who else?

PHILIP. Hmm? Oh—well no one—me I suppose.

JOANNA. You're working too hard these days. Is Henry doing his share?

PHILIP. Not 'arf. I mean he never stops—I mean yes. (Suddenly.) Darling, you do love me, don't me?

JOANNA. Silly. 'Course I do.

(Gives him a little hug and a kiss.)

PHILIP. But you wouldn't say I was a stick-in-the-mud, would you?

JOANNA. Yes.

PHILIP. Oh.

JOANNA (remembering HENRY and LINDA's complicated life). And that's exactly why I love you. And you're also gentle, calm and understanding. (She sits him on the sofa.)

PHILIP. You've never said that before.

JOANNA. Perhaps I've never felt it before.

(She gives him a long and lingering kiss.)

PHILIP. Mm, I enjoyed that. I think I *have* been working too hard lately. Wouldn't it be nice if we could forget this dreary dinner and have an early night?

JOANNA. Yes. (Suddenly.) God *no!*—God *knows* I'd like to but we can't, can we?

PHILIP. Can't we? (Sees HENRY's briefcase and quickly puts it behind sofa.) No, we can't! What are you wearing tonight?

JOANNA. I couldn't make up my mind so I went out and bought a couple of new dresses.

PHILIP (laughing). Two new dresses. That's not like you, well done. You can put that old black one out to grass now. Any other excitements?

JOANNA (gabbling guiltily). No nothing, not a soul, very quiet, no nobody came not even a visitor, very quiet. Look I'll go and run a drink, you pour yourself a bath—have a drink. Finish mine if you like before you get changed.

PHILIP. Yes, but we ought to be out by eight.

JOANNA (moving to dressing room.) Or seven forty-five.

PHILIP. Or even sooner.

JOANNA. Even better.

(She exits into dressing room taking the dress off the bed. PHILIP settles back. He puts his hand casually in between the sofa cushions and pulls out page 2 of LINDA's letter. (N.B. This is a duplicate page set before the rise of the curtain, for safety.) (He glances at it.)

PHILIP (reading casually). "Left me completely breath-less—"

(HENRY enters brightly from the study.)

HENRY. I don't know what you're on about. Spenlow seems to be doing a pretty good job in there.

PHILIP (reading aloud). ". . . sheer perfection . . . difficult to get away with a husband etc."

HENRY. What have you got there, old boy?

PHILIP. Dunno. Found it down between the cushions.

HENRY (takes it and reads). Page two. Where's one and three?

PHILIP. I don't know.

HENRY. ". . . breathless—What can one say about moments like that . . . husband etc. but please try to arrange something . . . I quite fancy the idea of trying . . ." (He starts to chuckle at the implications.) You sure you can't find page three?

PHILIP. What do you think it is?

HENRY. Well it's certainly not chapter two of Winnie The Pooh!

PHILIP. Do you know what I think? I'd say it's part of a love letter.

HENRY. Well done!

(HENRY gives PHILIP letter)

PHILIP. I think it's disgraceful—Miss Hauser receiving letters like this.

HENRY. That's not been written to Sylvie.

PHILIP. How can you tell?

HENRY (points to letter.) "Difficult to get away with a *husband* etc."

PHILIP. Oh yes. Well, who else could it be? (HENRY doesn't reply, merely places a consoling hand on PHILIP's shoulder, it dawns on him what HENRY means.) You don't mean Joanna?

HENRY. Who else? Probably not serious. Just a bit of slap and tickle.

PHILIP. Slap and tick . . .?

HENRY. Hurry up and offer me a drink, you've got to be shoving off soon.

PHILIP. Just a minute, you can't make slanderous remarks

like that. I mean ... er ... (he flounders). Even if it was written to Joanna the wording's very ambiguous. Could just be a "thank you" letter.

HENRY. That's exactly what it is.

PHILIP. Anyway, there's nothing to suggest it's from a chap at all. (HENRY gives him a look.) Could be from the woman who runs that Cordon Bleu cookery class.

HENRY. Couched in those terms?

PHILIP. They're a very arty flamboyant lot. Makes perfect sense. Your—er—chocolate mousse—"left me completely breathless"!

HENRY. Philip, I've tasted Joanna's mousse.

PHILIP. Dammit, if she's having lessons she might be getting better. (Refers to letter.) Yes, she obviously is, "Sheer perfection".

HENRY (sarcastically). I see.

PHILIP. "I know how difficult it is for you to get away with a husband etc."

HENRY. Charming, isn't it? You're in with the 'et ceteras'.

PHILIP. "But please try to arrange something." That'll be the next lesson. (HENRY just nods.) "I quite fancy the idea of trying—"

HENRY. Your apple crumble? Philip, please.

(HENRY takes the page back as ALISTAIR enters.)

ALISTAIR. Now about the lining for these cur—
PHILIP (rounding on him). Get out!!

(ALISTAIR about turns and exits.)

HENRY. Steady on, old man.

(ALISTAIR re-enters.)

ALISTAIR. It's going to be powder blue so there!

(PHILIP starts to rush at him and ALISTAIR shoots off.)

PHILIP. It can't be Joanna.

HENRY. Sort it out after your dinner, will you? We've got things to do tonight, remember? Miss Wilkinson.

PHILIP. You stand there accusing my—who's Miss Wilkinson?

HENRY. The operator who got me my personal call.

PHILIP. You stand there accusing my wife of being unfaithful and all you can think about is your telephone girl.

HENRY (glancing at his watch). Yes, you're right. If a wife's going off the rails there are plenty of signs. You'd have to be an idiot not to notice. So forget it and—

PHILIP. Signs? What sort of signs?

HENRY. Well you know, it affects them in different ways. Some women rush out and buy new clothes.

PHILIP. God. (Clutches HENRY.)

HENRY. What?

PHILIP. Two new dresses this very afternoon.

HENRY. Other women become over affectionate towards their husbands.

PHILIP (clutches HENRY again). That's it. Practically seduced me only five minutes ago. I can't believe it, Henry, I mean I've always given her whatever she wanted. I let her bring in that wretched decorator who's lumbered us with everything from a long-playing bell to an oval bed.

HENRY. I meant to ask you about that bed. Can you buy oval sheets?

PHILIP. No! (returning to the letter problem). What am I going to do?

HENRY. I should try square ones and fold the corners in.

(PHILIP throws up his hands in despair.)

PHILIP. What other signs would there be?

HENRY. Let's see er—pickled onions at three in the morning.

PHILIP. What?

HENRY. Oh no, that's the other thing.

PHILIP. Look, there's "new clothes", "over affectionate" what else?

HENRY. Does she get nervous for no apparent reason and laugh at nothing?

PHILIP. Laugh at nothing. No, I can't honestly say she's done that. But we've got two out of three. Give me that letter.

HENRY. Philip, it's seven thirty.

(JOANNA enters bedroom from dressing room, carrying a dress and a pair of shoes. She is wearing a flimsy dressing gown.)

PHILIP. Give me that letter. (He takes it.)

HENRY. What are you going to do?

PHILIP. I'm going to go in there, confront her with it and say—(he suddenly comes face to face with her as he opens the bedroom door). Hullo, darling! (He quickly stuffs the letter in his pocket.) What d'you want, what d'you want?

JOANNA. Nothing, I just came in to say—(suddenly sees HENRY) Henry!

HENRY. Yes?

JOANNA (nervously). How long have you been here?

HENRY. Few minutes.

JOANNA. Meet—er—anyone on the way in?

HENRY. No.

JOANNA. Good. Make sure you don't meet them on the way out.

(She starts to move him.)

HENRY (stopping). I was hoping for a drink actually.

JOANNA. Have mine.

(She takes the drink out of PHILIP's hand and gives it to HENRY.)

HENRY. I'm not too keen on gin.

JOANNA. Never mind. Just concentrate on the French.

(She gives a forced gay laugh. PHILIP looks from her to HENRY and back to her.)

PHILIP (flatly). What are you laughing at?

JOANNA (gaily). Nothing.

HENRY. Three out of three.

PHILIP (coldly). What did you want, darling?

JOANNA. Oh, well I just wanted to know what you felt about these. (She holds out the dress and the shoes.)

PHILIP. Conclusive.

HENRY (very quickly). Very, very pretty.

PHILIP. Are they new too?

JOANNA. Yes, I was wondering if they matched.

PHILIP (peering at each shoe). Yes, yes, I think so. Perfectly.

HENRY. With the dress.

PHILIP. Oh I see, yes. You've gone a bit mad today, haven't you, new dresses, new shoes—

JOANNA. That's nothing. I've bought some things for the flat as well. (She moves to the bedroom door.) They'll be sending them round from Harrods in the morning.

PHILIP. Sending what round? (Following her through into the bedroom.)

JOANNA. A dozen champagne glasses, a bamboo trolley and an enormous Ficus Elastica Decora.

PHILIP. What's that?

JOANNA. A rubber plant. (She laughs gaily and exits into dressing room.)

PHILIP. What about that?

HENRY. You've got no definite proof. I'd sleep on it.

PHILIP. Did you see her eyes, sparkling like billy-o.

HENRY. She's been shopping at Harrods.

PHILIP. That's not been brought on by a bamboo trolley, or an elasticated aspidistra.

(He marches straight into the bedroom and lays the letter on the bed.)

HENRY. For God's sake, what are you doing?

PHILIP. Getting my proof.

HENRY. What?

PHILIP. Look, if she's innocent she'll wonder what it is.

HENRY. And if she's guilty?

PHILIP. We'll soon see.

(By now he has got back into the sitting room and shut the door. He bends down and looks through the louvres.)

HENRY. What can you see?

PHILIP. The ceiling. (He looks through the keyhole.)

HENRY. What d'you hope to gain from all this?

PHILIP. A good view of my wife.

HENRY. Move over!

(He pushes PHILIP to one side and looks through the keyhole.)

PHILIP. Dammit, she's my wife.
HENRY. I'm your best friend.

(As they jostle each other at the keyhole, ALISTAIR enters from the study with two gaudy cushions. He stops abruptly on seeing the two men. His initial look of surprise changes into one of utter amazement as the implications click through his mind. He tiptoes out looking very shocked.)

HENRY (cont.). She might not come out again.
PHILIP. You don't know Joanna, there'll be ten minutes toing and froing before she takes her shower.
HENRY. You sure?
PHILIP. We've got rollers, cold cream, umpteen powders and 57 varieties of sprays.
HENRY. You should see Linda at night, it's like going to bed with a waffle machine.

(JOANNA enters bedroom and moves towards sitting room door.)

PHILIP. Yes, I know what you mean.

(They are just getting their eyes level with the keyhole again as JOANNA opens the door. The two men drop like stones on to their knees and pretend to be searching the floor.)

JOANNA (as she enters the living room). Darling, have you seen . . . (She stops on seeing the men at her feet.) Have you lost something?
HENRY. Yes, rather.
PHILIP. Yes.
HENRY: ⎱ (Together.) A sixpence.
PHILIP. ⎰ A cuff link.

HENRY. ⎫ (Together.) A cuff link.
PHILIP. ⎭ A sixpence.
PHILIP. A sixpenny cuff link.
JOANNA. Oh.

(She starts to look for it.)

PHILIP. Not worth bothering about. What did you want?
JOANNA. My spray.
PHILIP. Which spray?
JOANNA. Deodorant, have you had it?
PHILIP. No, I haven't.
JOANNA. That's right, you gave up borrowing it after you used my hair lacquer spray by mistake. You should have seen him, Henry. (She sticks both her arms out sideways, laughs, sees deodorant on window sill, picks it up and continues to bedroom still with arms extended.)

(She goes back into the bedroom and straight on through into the dressing room. PHILIP closes the door and he and HENRY kneel down again.)

HENRY. I don't get it, old man, why should hair lacquer make your arms stick out?
PHILIP (chuckling). Well, you see the spray makes—(stops chuckling). Never mind about that! Just let's concentrate on what we're doing.

(ALISTAIR enters from study and hears this last remark.)

HENRY. It was because you were talking she nearly caught us the last time.

(ALISTAIR is riveted once more.)

HENRY (cont.). Get your head over, I want to see as much as you.
PHILIP. Alright, alright, but it was my idea.
HENRY. Honestly, I think you're making a mistake. Especially doing it like this.

(ALISTAIR reacts.)

PHILIP. She's the one who put us in this position.

(ALISTAIR reacts.)

HENRY. What do you think she'll do?
PHILIP. Ssssh! I wish I'd done what I said I was going to do.
HENRY. What?
PHILIP. Gone in there and shown it to her.

(ALISTAIR looks horrified as SYLVIE enters from hall.)

SYLVIE. Mrs. Markham—
ALISTAIR ⎫
HENRY   ⎬ (together). Ahh!!
PHILIP   ⎭

(HENRY and PHILIP immediately leap to their feet. They then quickly drop to their knees again, searching. ALISTAIR, thoroughly confused, drops to his knees at the same time. The two men glare at him and he gets up.)

PHILIP. What do you want, Sylvie?
SYLVIE. I am going out soon, I wanted to ask Mrs. Markham if there was anything else she wanted.
PHILIP. No, she doesn't, she's very busy in the bedroom.
SYLVIE. You also are going out, yes?
PHILIP. Yes.
SYLVIE. Good. I shall say good night before I go.
PHILIP. Thank you very much.
SYLVIE. Not at all.

(As she passes ALISTAIR she gives him a quick goose.)

ALISTAIR (yells). Ahh!

(SYLVIE exits hallway as the other two men turn to look at ALISTAIR.)

HENRY. What's the matter with you?

ALISTAIR (quickly). Nothing. Didn't see a thing. I mean can't see it anywhere. (Glances at the desk.) My tape measure. Ah, there it is. (He grabs it off the desk.) Thanks very much. (Then pointedly.) Please don't get up.

(Alistair exits into the study. PHILIP immediately goes back to the keyhole. HENRY reluctantly follows him.)

PHILIP. Hope we haven't missed her. No, the letter's still there.

HENRY (looks at watch and sighs). Oh, my God.

PHILIP. What I don't understand, Henry, is why.

HENRY. Why what?

PHILIP. Why she's being unfaithful after fifteen years.

HENRY. I don't know. I suppose if you're dissatisfied with your baker you get your rolls elsewhere.

PHILIP (slowly looks at him). That is positively slanderous. There's never been any problem at all with our—"S-E-X". Hit it off from the word go. Doubt if there's been another honeymoon like it.

HENRY. That was fifteen years ago.

PHILIP. Yes.

HENRY. What about now?

PHILIP. Fine.

HENRY. Jolly good. How often, daily?

PHILIP (embarrassed). Henry.

HENRY. Quarterly.

PHILIP. Henry, please.

HENRY. Well how often?

PHILIP. For God's sake, I don't clock in!

HENRY. I see, annually.

PHILIP. The point is I've been faithful for fifteen years.

HENRY. I should say that's your trouble. You're as dreary now as you were then.

PHILIP. Now look here—

(The telephone rings.)

PHILIP (cont.). Oh hell. Let it ring.

(The telephone rings for a few more seconds.)

PHILIP (cont.). Might be important, better answer it.

(He moves to the telephone as JOANNA comes into the bedroom wearing a towelling dressing gown and an attractive shower hat.)

HENRY. Quick, she's back.

(PHILIP rushes back to the door. JOANNA glances in the direction of the living room, frowns, then lifts the receiver.)

JOANNA (into phone). 5970 . . . who? . . . Miss Smythe . . . well he was, but I think he must have popped out for a minute . . . certainly. Hang on, I'll just find something to write on, I'm a bit wet . . . I said I'm a bit—oh, it doesn't matter.

(She leans across and picks up the incriminating letter from the bed. Without looking at it she turns it over, takes a pen from the dressing table, and writes. PHILIP and HENRY react to this.)

JOANNA (cont.). Now (into phone) Smythe how are you spelling that? . . . S-M-Y-T-H-E, and the number? . . . oh Claridges I see. Right. Thank you. I'll tell him. Goodbye.

(She replaces the receiver. With the letter in her hand, she moves towards the sitting room door. PHILIP and HENRY scramble to the sofa and sit as nonchalantly as they can.)

JOANNA (cont.). Philip. (Entering the living room and stops on seeing HENRY, nervously.) You're still here, Henry.
HENRY. Yes.
JOANNA (gives a nervous laugh.) Oh, jolly good.

(The two men react to her laughter.)

JOANNA (cont.). I've got a message here. Didn't either of you hear the phone?
PHILIP \
        } (together). No
HENRY /

(During the ensuing dialogue PHILIP never takes his eye off the letter.)

JOANNA. Oh honestly.

PHILIP. What about the message? (Pointing to the letter.)

JOANNA. Ring a Miss Smythe at Claridges by eight o'clock.

(Moving back to the bedroom followed by PHILIP.)

PHILIP. Claridges at eight, yes.

JOANNA. And if the phone goes again, answer it. I'm trying to dry myself. Now where's the wastepaper thing?

(She screws the letter up, throws it out of the window and exits into dressing room.)

PHILIP. Ah!

HENRY. What is it?

PHILIP. My only bit of evidence, straight out of the window.

(He rushes to the window.)

HENRY (following him.) Come back.

PHILIP (leaning out of the window.) There it is, there it is! In the middle of the road.

HENRY. In the rush hour, just your luck.

PHILIP. Taxi! Taxi! Follow that piece of paper . . . yes, you follow that— (turns to HENRY.) Charming. I'll go down and get it.

HENRY. It'll be half way to Hyde Park by now.

(PHILIP pushes HENRY towards the hall as LINDA enters with bottle of champagne. HENRY and LINDA come face to face, startled. HENRY immediately kisses her profusely. He then turns to PHILIP.)

HENRY (cont.). It's my wife.

PHILIP. So it is.

LINDA. What are you doing here, Henry?

HENRY. Just popped up to discuss the cover for "Harry the Hornet". Well, it's been a nice day, hasn't it?

LINDA. Yes there's a bit of a breeze blowing now though.

PHILIP. Breeze. (He glances back at the window.) My God! (To HENRY) My letter!

(PHILIP dashes out into the hall.)

LINDA. What's wrong with Philip?
HENRY. Wind.

(JOANNA enters from the dressing room still in her
bathrobe and goes towards the living room.)

JOANNA. Philip. Do you want me to run a bath for you?
(Suddenly sees LINDA.) Linda!
LINDA. No thank you.
JOANNA. What a pleasant surprise. (She gives her false
laugh.) What are you doing here?
HENRY (innocently). Yes, what are you doing here?
LINDA. Popped in to see Joanna.
HENRY. Who's the champagne for?
LINDA (handing it to JOANNA). Happy birthday, darling.
JOANNA (thoroughly confused). Thank you.
HENRY (with cheerful surprise). You never told me it was
your birthday.
JOANNA (gabbling). Ah, no, well, you see, I hadn't, there
wasn't, she didn't, I couldn't, you mustn't. (She stops and
giggles.)
LINDA. Are you staying long, Henry?
HENRY. No, no, just settling this book question with
Philip.
JOANNA. Where is he?
HENRY. Just popped down to er—er—
JOANNA. The office?
HENRY. Yes, that'll do. Be back soon. (Nervously.) D'you
mind if I pour myself that whisky, Jo?
JOANNA. No, go ahead.
HENRY. Can I get something for you?
LINDA. No, thank you.

(She pushes him into the bar and closes the door.)

JOANNA. You're not due till 8.30!
LINDA. I wanted to put the champagne on ice. Do it for
me, will you? I'll nip home and change into something
promising. Oh—where do you keep the tea?
JOANNA. Tea?

LINDA. I can't do a thing till I've had a cup of tea.

(The telephone rings and JOANNA picks up the receiver.)

JOANNA. 5970 . . . Yes, this is Mrs. Markham speaking . . . Walter who? Walter!

LINDA. Walter!?

HENRY (pops his head into the room). No, it's alright, I prefer soda. (He disappears again.)

JOANNA. Yes, she is as it happens . . . (to LINDA.) He wants to speak to you. He must be mad.

LINDA. I expect he's getting impatient, I'll take it in the bedroom. (She rushes through, closing bedroom door.)

JOANNA (sarcastically). Hold the line one moment please, I'm trying to connect you.

LINDA (on phone). What is it, my dolly Wally Walter?

JOANNA. Oh, whoopee!

(JOANNA replaces receiver and places champagne on desk.)

LINDA (on phone). Yes, it's all arranged, my sweet.

(HENRY enters from bar. During the ensuing dialogue LINDA curls up on the bed with back to audience and we don't hear her conversation.)

HENRY. Mustn't be too long, Linda, I—oh, where is she?

JOANNA. On the phone.

HENRY. I thought *you* were.

JOANNA. No, I finished mine. She suddenly remembered she hadn't rung Uncle lately.

HENRY. Oh I see. Which Uncle?

JOANNA. Have you got an Uncle George?

HENRY. Yes.

JOANNA. That's the one!

HENRY. Poor old Uncle George. He's been under the weather lately.

(He moves towards the bedroom with an anxious JOANNA following him. LINDA has now turned round on the bed and is making kissing noises to WALTER on the phone. Unseen by LINDA, HENRY enters behind her and smiles at her solicitous attitude towards 'Uncle George'.)

HENRY (cont.) (finally). Give him my love.
LINDA (flustered). What?
HENRY. Tell him to keep his pecker up.
LINDA. Pecker up?
HENRY. Uncle George.
LINDA. Oh, yes– (on phone). No, no, it's Henry . . . your *nephew* . . . my *husband*– Henry! . . . H-E-N–
HENRY. Hang on– (moving). Let me have a word.
LINDA. 'Bye, Uncle George. The pips went. (She bangs phone down and gives it to HENRY. She hurries through into sitting room.)
HENRY. Pips, he only lives in Putney. (He comes through into sitting room.)
LINDA. 'Bye, Jo darling. See you over the weekend maybe. (Then quietly.) Leave the front door on the latch. (Louder.) See you at home, Henry.
HENRY. No. I forgot to mention, I'm out this evening.
LINDA. Oh pity.
HENRY. Yes, usual thing.
HENRY ⎫ (together) Entertaining an important client.
LINDA ⎭
HENRY. 'Fraid so, yes.
JOANNA. Who is it, Henry?
HENRY. Mm? Oh, an elderly schoolmaster. From Harrow.
JOANNA. Oh.
HENRY (to LINDA). He–er–fancies himself as a bit of a storyteller.
LINDA. Ah.

(The girls exchange a knowing smile.)

HENRY. Got this–er–exciting idea. About a tortoise.
LINDA. Really.
HENRY. Bill Humphreys.
JOANNA. Extraordinary name for a tortoise.
HENRY. Yes–no, that's the name of the author. We haven't decided on a name for the tortoise, in fact that's one of the reasons we're meeting tonight. I haven't actually met this–er–

LINDA. Bill Humphreys.

HENRY. Thank you, well, when I say we haven't met, we've chatted over the phone quite a bit. He's full of ideas. I should think we may be in for a lengthy do tonight.

JOANNA. Well don't over-do it, Henry.

HENRY. No-no I won't. (To LINDA.) You needn't wait up for me.

LINDA. Matter of fact I—er—I may be late myself tonight.

HENRY. Oh really.

LINDA. I'm out too.

HENRY (surprised). Are you?

LINDA. I'll be busy until about—

JOANNA. Ten-thirty.

LINDA. Ten-thirty.

HENRY. What is it?

LINDA. Joanna's persuaded me to do something for charity.

HENRY. Have you, Jo, splendid. Don't exhaust yourself.

LINDA. It's all in a good cause.

HENRY. Really, what?

JOANNA. Undeveloped Areas.

(LINDA gives JOANNA a quick kiss and goes as PHILIP enters in a temper.)

LINDA. Hullo, Philip, can't stop, how's your tummy?

PHILIP. Bloody awful.

JOANNA. Philip—

(She ushers LINDA out.)

JOANNA (cont.). Must be his ulcer, he's always like this when he's rushed . . .

(The girls disappear.)

HENRY. What's happened?

PHILIP. I'm being questioned by the Police.

HENRY. What about?

PHILIP. Moving a vehicle that was not legally in my possession.

HENRY. Why?

PHILIP. Damn letter blew into the gutter—car parked on

it—owner walked away—couldn't stop him—couldn't pull letter out from under wheel—got into car—arrested.

HENRY. Oh really, Philip. You are thoughtless. What about my Miss Wilkinson, she's waiting for me to ring her and tell her to come round here.

PHILIP. Never mind Miss Wilkinson, I've got a domestic crisis in here and an angry policeman waiting outside.

HENRY. What for?

PHILIP. He wanted to see some means of identity.

HENRY. You've got a licence or something.

PHILIP. Yes, in the drawer. (He goes to the desk.)

HENRY. Where is this constable?

PHILIP. In the main hall.

HENRY. I'll go and sort it out.

PHILIP. That should get me eighteen months at least.

HENRY. You and your damn letter.

PHILIP. And there's not much left of that.

(He pulls a torn and oily strip of the letter out of his pocket.)

PHILIP (cont.). My last shred of evidence in shreds.

(HENRY takes PHILIP's arm.)

HENRY. Good. We'll deal with the law, then you can get ready and clear off.

(They move towards the hall. ALISTAIR enters again with two gaudy cushions.)

ALISTAIR. Frightfully sorry to butt in, but if I don't get—
PHILIP. Not now. We're engaged.
ALISTAIR (raises an eyebrow). Lovely.
PHILIP. This is urgent.
HENRY. We're in a spot of bother with the police.
ALISTAIR. I see!

(They give him a look and are about to exit as JOANNA re-enters.)

JOANNA. Hurry up, Philip. It's high time we were getting dressed.

PHILIP (rounding on his "unfaithful" wife). I'll get dressed when I feel like it.

HENRY. Steady old man.

PHILIP. And not before.

JOANNA (puzzled). Darling.

HENRY. You mustn't talk to your wife like that.

PHILIP. Oh mustn't I.

HENRY. Especially on her birthday.

(PHILIP does a double-take as HENRY pushes him off into hall.)

PHILIP. Birthday?

(They exit.)

ALISTAIR. Now about these cushions.

JOANNA. They look goegeous, scatter them round.

ALISTAIR. No. They're for the "master's" study but he won't give me an opinion.

JOANNA. Oh, they're far too gaudy for him. Anyway I shouldn't press the point, he's not in one of his gay moods.

ALISTAIR (pointedly). Oh, I don't know.

JOANNA. He's had a busy day. Discuss it with him tomorrow. Goodnight, Alistair.

ALISTAIR. Oh, Mrs. Markham, didn't I mention?

JOANNA. What?

ALISTAIR. I'm working late tonight.

JOANNA (worried). Where?

ALISTAIR. Here.

JOANNA. No!

ALISTAIR. What?

JOANNA. No. You can't . . . I mean you mustn't.

ALISTAIR. I've got one or two things to round off.

JOANNA. But we're all going out.

ALISTAIR. Lovely. I won't be disturbed.

JOANNA. Yes, you will. I mean you might. I mean *you* might disturb *other people.*

ALISTAIR. What other people?

JOANNA. Underneath.

ALISTAIR. I'm only hanging curtains, dear.

JOANNA. It's awfully heavy material though. Why don't you give yourself a rest.

(She sits him on pouffe down left.)

ALISTAIR. But, I feel fine.

JOANNA. No, Alistair. I don't want you to stay here tonight.

ALISTAIR. Why not?

JOANNA. Because—because we want you to come with us—to the publishers' dinner. As our guest.

ALISTAIR. The publishers' dinner?

JOANNA. It's my husband's idea, actually.

ALISTAIR (suspiciously). Is it?

JOANNA. Yes. Believe it or not he's taken quite a fancy to you.

ALISTAIR. Has he?!

(PHILIP and HENRY enter.)

PHILIP. But Henry, I keep telling you, you don't offer policemen bribes.

HENRY. I thought it would be alright.

PHILIP. And certainly not two bob.

HENRY. He went away happily enough. (The phone rings.)

PHILIP. Oh, that damn phone.

JOANNA. No, no—I'll get it. (Laughs.)

(JOANNA goes to answer it and during the ensuing scene PHILIP keeps a beady on her.)

JOANNA (lifts the receiver). 5970 . . . Yes he is actually . . . It's for you, Henry.

HENRY (casually). Me?

JOANNA. It's the operator. Something about a personal call.

HENRY. I haven't booked a— (realising). Personal call?! (He grabs the phone and puts his hand over the mouthpiece as he explains to JOANNA.) It'll be New York. I booked a call earlier, we're trying to get the British rights of Yogi Bear.

PHILIP (tetchily). Good luck.

HENRY. Thanks. (Into phone.) Hullo, operator, Lodge here . . . oh yes, I was going to ring you but I was delayed . . . yes, I still want it! . . . Well bearing in mind the time lag, better make it eight fifteen . . . I'll be waiting. G'bye. (He replaces the receiver.) I think Yogi Bear's in the bag.

ALISTAIR. Mr. Markham, if I could just—

PHILIP (sharply). What do you want?

ALISTAIR. Oh, well your wife considers these cushions are too gaudy for your study.

PHILIP (still glaring at JOANNA). Does she?

JOANNA. I just thought they might clash with what Alistair's already done in there.

PHILIP. Very likely, so he can change what he's done. (Being difficult.) I like these cushions. I love them. And I want them on a black Swedish settee, preferably leather, with a crimson carpet and orange plastic curtains. (To ALISTAIR.) How d'you feel about that?

ALISTAIR. Yuk!

JOANNA. Darling, you've got to be joking.

PHILIP. I couldn't be more serious.

JOANNA. Doesn't sound very like you, Philip.

PHILIP (with a brittle smile). We learn something fresh about each other every day, don't we, darling?

JOANNA. Yes—we certainly do. Pay no attention to him, Alistair.

PHILIP (petulantly). I want my black Swedish settee, my plastic curtains and crimson carpet.

JOANNA (tapping her watch). Philip, it's seven thirty.

HENRY. Precisely.

PHILIP. So what?

JOANNA. In another half hour it'll be eight o'clock.

PHILIP. Higher mathematics was always her strong point.

JOANNA. All I'm saying is we've got to get ready for dinner and Henry's got to meet Bill.

HENRY (blankly). Bill?

JOANNA. That tortoise author.

HENRY. Oh yes, of course, Bill Humphreys.

JOANNA (to PHILIP). Oh, and I forgot to tell you I've asked Alistair to come with us to the dinner.

PHILIP. Alistair? What on earth for?

JOANNA. Company.

PHILIP. I get quite enough of his company here.

ALISTAIR. Don't worry, I'm working late tonight.

JOANNA. No, you aren't!

HENRY. No, you aren't!

JOANNA. The point is, darling, you mustn't be late.

PHILIP. Oh, mustn't I? It's amazing the way people take me for granted. I shall be late if I want to. Lot of things I want to discuss.

ALISTAIR. Super. Now about the study—

PHILIP. That's settled, thank you, Mr. Spenlow. Crimson curtains, orange leather settee and black plastic carpet. (They all react to his getting it muddled up.)

ALISTAIR. Is there anything else?

PHILIP. Yes. I want something to match your chiming bell.

ALISTAIR (rather pleased). Oh, really?

PHILIP. A musical lavatory flush.

JOANNA. Now please, darling. Just leave it to Alistair.

PHILIP. I'm perfectly capable of making my own artistic decisions.

ALISTAIR (angry). Yes. A musical—I suppose you wouldn't like a flight of ducks up your bathroom wall.

PHILIP. Lovely.

HENRY (blandly). And you can have one of those little stone fellows fishing in the—

PHILIP. Oh, shut up.

ALISTAIR. It's a pity you didn't show a little more interest earlier on.

PHILIP. Well, I'm making up for it now.

ALISTAIR. I thought your wife had got carte blanche.

PHILIP. Did you? Well she hasn't!

HENRY. Steady.

JOANNA. You get ready, dear, and you can have anything you want.

PHILIP. Thank you. (Dramatically.) I'll have the evening at home.

JOANNA. At home!?

HENRY. No you can't!

JOANNA. No you can't!

ALISTAIR. No you can't!

PHILIP (to ALISTAIR). What's it got to do with you?

ALISTAIR. Nothing at all.

PHILIP (to JOANNA). We're staying in tonight. What have you got to say to that?

JOANNA (picking up the receiver). I think I'll ring Linda.

PHILIP (to JOANNA). What's it got to do with Linda?

JOANNA. Nothing. That's just what I'm going to tell her. (Sees HENRY and laughs foolishly.) In the bedroom.

(She bangs down the receiver and goes hurriedly into the bedroom. During the ensuing dialogue she dials the number with her back to the audience.)

ALISTAIR (furiously). I'm sick to death of people changing their minds around here!

HENRY. Alright, don't get your knickers in a twist.

ALISTAIR. Oh!

HENRY (whispering). For God's sake, Phil, what about my operator?

PHILIP (whispering). I've got my own problems.

HENRY (whispering). Miss Wilkinson's coming here at 8.15!

(ALISTAIR has approached them.)

ALISTAIR. More little secrets?

HENRY. No, it's about this fellow I'm meeting this evening.

ALISTAIR. Oh yes. Bill Humphreys.

HENRY. Oh well if we can't use this place we'll just have to go dancing.

ALISTAIR (puckishly). Oh! (He throws his cushions gaily in the air.)

PHILIP. Need you stay, Spenlow?

ALISTAIR. Yes, I've got plenty to be getting on with.

PHILIP. You can forget coming out to dinner with us.

ALISTAIR. Thank you. (He collects up his cushions off the floor.)

HENRY. I better cancel Miss Wilkinson. Is Joanna off the phone yet?

(He moves to the bedroom while we hear the end of JOANNA's conversation. She is walking with the phone towards the living room door.)

JOANNA. . . . Well get Mrs. Lodge to ring me the moment she comes in. Tell her it's vital and absolutely—(sees HENRY as he opens the bedroom door) unimportant. (She replaces the receiver.)

HENRY. Can I use the phone?

JOANNA. No. (Laughs.) Not yet. (Then pressing on nervously.) Have you settled the orange plastic question, Alistair?

ALISTAIR. No, but if Mr. Markham's going to change all my colour schemes I'm going down to the car to fetch some more catalogues.

PHILIP. Don't bother.

(The telephone, still in JOANNA's hand, rings. She and HENRY look at it suspiciously, neither of them cares to find out who it is, so try to ignore it and smile at each other, hoping that it'll stop ringing.)

PHILIP (cont.) (eventually). Is everybody deaf or something?

(He takes off the receiver.)

PHILIP (cont.) (on phone, curtly). Hullo . . . who? . . . Miss Smythe? Oh no, I hadn't forgotten, I'm a bit involved at the moment . . . You've written a children's book? I'd love to . . . Claridges, yes, I'll ring you. (He replaces the receiver.)
ALISTAIR. I'll get those catalogues.
PHILIP. Nobody wants you to do anything more tonight.
ALISTAIR. That's what you think.
JOANNA. Forget about the catalogues. I'll come over to your studio in the morning.
ALISTAIR. It's alright, I'm going to do it now. (Pointedly referring to PHILIP.) I know it isn't easy for you to get away with a husband, etc.

(He exits. PHILIP, on hearing ALISTAIR use the phrase from the letter, is aghast. He moves, almost in a trance, towards the hall, looking after ALISTAIR.)

JOANNA. I'm going to get dressed. You're quite sure you won't change your mind about staying in, darling?
PHILIP (his thoughts still on the letter.) "Not easy to get away".
JOANNA. Alright, but I can't see why.
HENRY. No, neither can I. Lend me the phone, Jo.

(He makes a move to take the phone from her.)

JOANNA (quickly). No, that's mine. I want to have a tinkle in the bathroom. (She exits into dressing room, taking the phone with her.)
PHILIP. Did you hear that?
HENRY. Yes, she said she wanted to have a tinkle in the—

PHILIP. No. "Not easy to get away with a husband, etc."

HENRY. Hmm?

PHILIP. Those were Spenlow's exact words just now.

HENRY. Were they?

PHILIP (taking out the remains of the letter). In the letter, too.

HENRY. Oh, yes.

(They both glance at the grubby scrap of paper.)

HENRY (cont.). Blessed if it's there now.

PHILIP. That's why he's been here three months. Talk about piece-work. Be warned. Next time you want new curtains run 'em up yourself.

HENRY. Can't be Spenlow.

PHILIP. He used the exact phrase. My wife at it, left, right and centre with the builder.

HENRY. Shh!

PHILIP. No wonder she invited him to dinner, can't be parted for ten minutes.

HENRY. You've got no evidence now that letter's been destroyed.

PHILIP. Wait a minute. The rest of it may be in her handbag.

(He picks it up from the desk and looks through it.)

HENRY. You're making a damn fool of yourself.

PHILIP. They've already done that.

HENRY. Is there any sign of it?

PHILIP. No I'm afraid there isn't. Oh, very frustrating.

(Marches angrily up and down clutching the handbag.)

PHILIP (cont.) (ignoring HENRY.) While I'm down on the ground floor reading "Tales for Tiny Tots" Joanna and Spenlow are up here bouncing about on my oval bed.

HENRY. I don't believe it.

PHILIP. That's it. Downstairs, infancy. Upstairs, adultery.

HENRY. I'm sure it's not Spenlow. (Chuckling.) He's one of those, isn't he?

PHILIP. One of which?

HENRY. Well—them—you know.

PHILIP. What?

HENRY. Pouf—queer.

(He puts his hand limply on his hip, takes a few mincing steps just as ALISTAIR enters from the hall carrying an armful of catalogues and samples. ALISTAIR stops and stares at HENRY, who quickly comes out of his pose, sits and takes out his pipe to prove his manhood. ALISTAIR then turns towards PHILIP who is still holding the handbag. ALISTAIR does a doubletake. PHILIP reacts to the handbag and furiously chucks it on the desk.)

PHILIP. Now I want a word with you, Spenlow.

ALISTAIR (struggling with heavy catalogues). Good, I've got everything, including a double hernia.

PHILIP. Been straining yourself, have you?

ALISTAIR. I certainly have.

(He spreads everything out on the table.)

HENRY. I'd better cancel Miss Wilkinson. I'll go down and ring her from the office. Don't rush into anything.

(He exits.)

ALISTAIR. Before we discuss the frills perhaps we could settle the basic colour patterns.

PHILIP (gritting his teeth). Sounds like a good idea.

ALISTAIR (opening a catalogue). Now what colour do you wish to dominate the study?

PHILIP. Black.

ALISTAIR (slightly put out). I see. Well, that might clash with your idea about the settee. Now, let me show you these rather dolly contrasts. I've got the charts here.

(He shows them one by one to PHILIP who is still mentally strangling him as JOANNA enters into bedroom in a housecoat, carrying the phone and talking on it.)

JOANNA. . . . No, I'm sorry, Linda, not tonight . . . Well, you'll just have to ring Walter again and tell him you *can't* come here . . . I don't know, try the roof garden at Derry and Toms. 'Bye 'bye.

(She puts the phone down and then all smiles, opens the door into the living room and hurries through.)

JOANNA (cont.). Now my darlings, is everything alright.
ALISTAIR. I think so.
JOANNA (casually). Don't exhaust yourself. Well, if we're all staying in, I'll see if I can find something for us to eat.

(She innocently pats ALISTAIR's cheek and exits hall. Philip reacts and glares after her.)

ALISTAIR. You see, it all hinges on whether you use the room primarily by day or by night. It's entirely a question of lighting.

(During this speech PHILIP is checking to see that JOANNA has gone off.)

ALISTAIR (cont.). By this I mean will it be artificial or normal.

(PHILIP has by this time taken his courage in both hands.)

PHILIP. Are you, or are you not, a pouf?

(ALISTAIR's expression goes completely blank for several seconds, then he decides he must have misheard the question.)

ALISTAIR. If—(he clears his throat). If you're going to have mainly artificial light I would suggest dark colours. On the other hand—

(He stops and decides that after all perhaps he hasn't misheard—)

ALISTAIR (cont.). I beg your pardon?
PHILIP. Are you—(fumbles for the word) queer?

(There is a pause.)

ALISTAIR (in a very deep manly voice). Now this blue has a wonderful quality about it.

PHILIP. When I say queer, I don't mean—"queer". (He rubs his stomach.) I mean "queer". (Puts his hand awkwardly on his hip.) You with me?

ALISTAIR. Yes—No! Perhaps if we could just stick to the catalogues.

PHILIP. Now look here, Spenlow, I don't think you are, but my friend thinks there's no doubt about it.

ALISTAIR (bemused). Your friend?

PHILIP. Yes, Mr. Lodge.

ALISTAIR. Oh, *that* friend.

PHILIP. So I ask you again, and I can tell you your answer means an awful lot to me.

ALISTAIR (eases away a step or two). I would be grateful if er—

PHILIP. Look, I'm fairly convinced you know why I'm asking you, and if Mr. Lodge hadn't said take it gently, I'd probably go for you here and now!

(PHILIP makes a move towards ALISTAIR who quickly slams the catalogue shut, gathers his things together and moves as far away as he can.)

ALISTAIR. Choose whatever colour you like and I won't charge you a penny.

PHILIP. Look, Spenlow. Please, I'd like to believe Mr. Lodge.

ALISTAIR. Really.

PHILIP. It would ease my mind if you're only a little bit queer!

ALISTAIR (rounding on him angrily). Mr. Markham—

PHILIP (hopefully). Even just fifty-fifty.

ALISTAIR. Fifty-fifty?!

PHILIP. Admit it. Go on. Please!

ALISTAIR. I can tell you, and you can tell your friend, that I am as normal as the next man. (Looks at PHILIP and steps away a pace.) I am one hundred per cent normal.

PHILIP (sits). Oh God, no.

ALISTAIR (rather concerned). Now, Mr. Markham, please.

PHILIP. Why did I listen to Henry, I knew I was right.

ALISTAIR. Plenty of other fish in the sea.

PHILIP (rises). Oh! You're callous, Spenlow.

(PHILIP moves upstage in anguish.)

ALISTAIR. I can't help the way I'm made.
PHILIP (groans). What a mess.

(Sinks his head in his hand. At the same time ALISTAIR bends down to pick up a dropped catalogue and SYLVIE enters from the hallway behind them, dressed to go out with a shoulder bag. She sees ALISTAIR bend to pick the catalogue up from the floor and gooses him.)

ALISTAIR (leaping up). Mr. Markham!

(SYLVIE looks in amazement. ALISTAIR is surprised to see it's SYLVIE and PHILIP looks round startled.)

PHILIP. You still here, Sylvie?
SYLVIE. I am going. Good night, Mr. Markham, see you in the morning. (PHILIP nods.) Good night, Mr. Spenlow, (Then whispers so that PHILIP doesn't hear.) See you later.

(She exits.)

ALISTAIR (without thinking). Yes. (Realises.) No!

(As he moves to follow her PHILIP steps in the way.)

PHILIP. You stay with me.
ALISTAIR (backs away). No—please. Discuss it in the morning.
PHILIP (rounding on him). We'll discuss it now. How long's it been going on?
ALISTAIR (blankly). I beg your pardon?
PHILIP. Look, I know what you've been up to these last twelve weeks.
ALISTAIR (baffled). Do you?
PHILIP. Indeed I do.
ALISTAIR. I've hung wallpaper, curtains, laid carpets—
PHILIP. And what *else* have you 'laid'?
ALISTAIR (innocently). Kitchen tiles, bathroom tiles—
PHILIP. You know what I mean. "Who" else?

ALISTAIR (thinking he means SYLVIE, relieved). Oh. (Points to hall.)

PHILIP. Yes!

ALISTAIR. You mean—

PHILIP. Yes. You filthy furnisher.

ALISTAIR (putting down his catalogues). Mr. Markham, I assure you I never let it interfere with my work.

PHILIP. Oh didn't you.

ALISTAIR. No. I never mix business with birds.

PHILIP. Birds! Well, if that doesn't take the biscuit. Did either of you ever stop to consider my feelings?

ALISTAIR. No, I can't honestly say we did.

PHILIP. I suppose it never occurred to you that I love her.

ALISTAIR. You?

PHILIP. Yes. Until today I never realised how much.

(He sits dejectedly.)

ALISTAIR (in disbelief). Gosh you're versatile.

(HENRY enters.)

HENRY. Missed her by five minutes. She's already on her way. I shall have to wait by the main door. (He sees PHILIP.) Everything alright?

PHILIP. No it's not. He's as guilty as hell and proud of it.

HENRY. Bit of a facer. I could've sworn he was a —

ALISTAIR. Well, I'm not!

HENRY. I apologise, most sincerely. (Goes to shake his hand.)

PHILIP (exploding). Don't apologise! Now come on, how long's it been going on?

ALISTAIR. Depends what you mean by "it". All I've done so far is to give her the occasional "goose".

(PHILIP looks at HENRY and then back at ALISTAIR.)

PHILIP (lost). In the middle of June?

ALISTAIR. No, no, I mean a friendly goose.

(PHILIP looks back at HENRY.)

HENRY. You know, a platonic goose.

(PHILIP looks back at ALISTAIR and ALISTAIR demonstrates a quick goose accompanied by a whistle, on an imaginary person.)

PHILIP. What's that supposed to be?

ALISTAIR. A goose.

PHILIP. D'you know what he's talking about?

HENRY. 'Course. I was stationed three years in Portsmouth.

PHILIP. Look, am I being dim, or what?

HENRY. Afraid you are a bit. It's the British version of the Continental bottom pinch.

PHILIP (irritably). What the devil's all this mean? (He waggles his hand and whistles.)

HENRY. Well, the whistle is optional but basically a goose is done by keeping the palm of the hand upwards—(he demonstrates) about three feet off the ground and then flicking the fingers quickly—so.

PHILIP. I don't get the point of that at all.

ALISTAIR. You would if you were standing over it.

PHILIP. Well, I've certainly never done it.

ALISTAIR. No, it doesn't really go with cream paint and mahogany. There are of course variations on—(he does it again)— there's an even craftier one—(he turns his hand backwards and does it to PHILIP, catching him in the behind.)

PHILIP (jumps). Oo! (Suddenly realising the situation regarding JOANNA, he turns on ALISTAIR.) And you've been doing that to her?

ALISTAIR. She started it.

PHILIP. What?

ALISTAIR. First week I was here, I bent down to—

PHILIP. I don't wish to know that! (To HENRY.) Have you ever heard anything so blatant?

HENRY. Doesn't sound too serious.

PHILIP. For those of us who haven't served in Portsmouth it sounds *bloody* serious. (To ALISTAIR.) No doubt you've progressed from all this goosing? How far did you intend to go?

ALISTAIR. All the way.

PHILIP (moves to hit him). Don't you get—

(HENRY quickly comes between them.)

HENRY. No violence, please.

PHILIP. I'll thump him!

ALISTAIR. Don't distress yourself, Mr. Markham, she just naturally prefers a younger man.

PHILIP (to HENRY). You're a witness to all this.

(PHILIP is consumed with anger as JOANNA enters from hall.)

JOANNA (cheerfully). Now, my Darlings, how many am I preparing for?

PHILIP. That's what we'd all like to know.

JOANNA. There's only Sylvie's sauerkraut and pumpernickel left.

HENRY (backing out). If I'm going to stop Miss Wilkinson—

PHILIP. You've got plenty of time. I want you here as a witness.

ALISTAIR (moving towards hall). You won't be needing me for a min—

PHILIP. Where the hell are you going?

ALISTAIR (about turns). Spend a penny. (Going through into bedroom).

PHILIP. That's my bathroom. (Following).

ALISTAIR. I installed it.

(ALISTAIR exits into dressing room.)

PHILIP. Be damn quick about it.

JOANNA. What's upset him, Henry?

PHILIP (turning back to her). You can drop that nonsense now, I'm not as silly as I look, you know.

JOANNA. Of course your not darling.

PHILIP. Fifteen years—!

HENRY. Remember my advice.

PHILIP. To hell with your advice. (To JOANNA.) Fifteen years we've been married and how often have you given me any of the—(mimes the goose) or the—(mimes it again backwards, whistling both times).

JOANNA. What's that?

PHILIP. A variety of geese.

JOANNA. Geese?

HENRY. Denotes affection.

PHILIP. She knows what it denotes. You've never given me one have you?

JOANNA. I didn't know you wanted one.

PHILIP. I don't. But you don't have to pepper the decorator with them.

JOANNA (bemused). Philip darling, what are you talking about?

PHILIP. You and that designer.

JOANNA. Alistair? What about him?

PHILIP. God, she's cool, Henry.

HENRY (trying to be kind). It's no good, Jo old love, he found the letter.

JOANNA. What letter?

PHILIP (pulling out the shred of paper and waggling it in front of her face). This erotic document.

JOANNA (still mystified and worried). I think I'll call the doctor, Henry.

(She moves to the phone and picks up the receiver.)

PHILIP. "Left me breathless, sheer perfection. I quite fancy the idea of trying—"

JOANNA. Ah! (She slams the phone down.)

PHILIP. Ahhhh.

JOANNA. Where did you find that?

PHILIP. Careless, weren't you?

JOANNA. It must have dropped—

PHILIP. Yes, it must have. How long's it been going on?

JOANNA. It's not even my—(sees HENRY beside her) my—my—my goodness! (She gives her silly laugh.) I'll explain later.

PHILIP. It's already been explained by your lover. (Points to the bathroom.)

JOANNA (bemused). Lover?

PHILIP. Spenlow the paperhanger.

HENRY. He confessed.

JOANNA. He must be mad.

PHILIP. Henry. Perhaps you'd give me a room for the night before I move into a hotel.

HENRY } We'll discuss it on the way down. }
JOANNA } Please, Philip darling— } together
You're being ridiculous. Henry, wait downstairs in the hall.

HENRY. Good idea.

PHILIP (stops him). You stay here. You're my only witness.

(ALISTAIR enters from the dressing room and walks through into the living room.)

PHILIP (cont.). There are still some of us left who believe in moral decency. (Sees ALISTAIR.) Ah, come in, my wife's ready, there's the bed, the pyjamas are under the pillow and the best of luck to you and Mother Goose.

ALISTAIR. Pardon?

JOANNA. Philip darling, please.

PHILIP. Don't touch me, you floosie! Come on, Henry, I'm going to find myself a young lady. I shall move out, Spenlow can move in and slosh his paintbrush wherever he likes!

(PHILIP and HENRY exit.)

ALISTAIR. Yes Well, I think I'll carry on in the study.

JOANNA. No. (Grabs his hand.) You'll carry on in the bed!

(She drags him towards the bedroom as the CURTAIN FALLS.)

ACT TWO

The action is continuous.

JOANNA is pursuing ALISTAIR around the bed.
ALISTAIR backs into the sitting room.

ALISTAIR. No, please, Mrs. Markham. I think you're
absolutely gorgeous, and I do appreciate your kind invitation—
JOANNA. You heard my husband, it's a definite offer.
ALISTAIR. Shouldn't we observe a few formalities.
JOANNA. Joanna Markham. How d'you do. (She shakes his
hand drags him back to the bedroom.) One blanket or two?
ALISTAIR (still rather flustered). Well I—er—I think one'll
be plenty for me, I get very hot—(quickly). Not unpleasantly
so.

(She removes and folds up the counterpane, revealing
orange sheets and pillow cases.)

JOANNA (businesslike). Pillows?
ALISTAIR. What if your husband—
JOANNA. Pillows!?
ALISTAIR. Yes, please.
JOANNA (impatiently). How many?
ALISTAIR. I'm just a little worried about your husb—
JOANNA. How many?!
ALISTAIR. One, please.
JOANNA. Pyjamas. (Thrusts them at him.)
ALISTAIR. No, thank you, I don't wear them—
JOANNA (taking them back instantly). Super!
ALISTAIR (grabs them equally quickly). Usually! However
under—the—under one blanket I might get a bit chilly.
JOANNA (suddenly going in close to him). Chilly?
ALISTAIR. You're sure your husband wasn't joking?
JOANNA. Positive.

(She starts to remove his jacket and tie, dropping them
on the floor.)

JOANNA (cont.). Which side of the bed do you generally have, left or right?

ALISTAIR. The middle. Oh I see—I don't mind really.

JOANNA. I prefer the left, is that alright?

ALISTAIR. Fine, yes, if you've been sleeping that way for years—well not years exactly.

JOANNA. Come on, trousers, trousers.

ALISTAIR (backing into the living room and taking off his shoes at the same time). Alright, alright. You're sure you won't regret any of this?

JOANNA (still breezy). Can't wait. How about you?

ALISTAIR. Raring to go. (Removing his trousers.)

JOANNA. That's the ticket!

(She turns and reacts to his gaily coloured underpants.)

JOANNA (cont.). Come on, beddy-byes.

ALISTAIR (stops dead). Ah!

JOANNA. What now?

ALISTAIR. Sylvie!

JOANNA. She's gone out.

ALISTAIR. But she's coming back. I mean she could be coming back.

JOANNA. Not before twelve, anyway.

ALISTAIR. Yes she will—she might. We don't want to be disturbed.

JOANNA. Do you want to come to bed or not?

(ALISTAIR weighs up the pros and cons and looks at his watch.)

ALISTAIR. Yes!

JOANNA. Are you quite sure you can spare the time?

ALISTAIR. Yes. Absolutely. A bird in the hand is—I'll leave a note on the door.

(He dashes to the desk and scribbles a note.)

JOANNA. Tell her I don't want to be disturbed. I'll find a nightie.

ALISTAIR. Gorgeous.

JOANNA (losing her courage slightly). Now you're quite certain about this?

ALISTAIR. You bet.

JOANNA. I wouldn't want you to have any feelings of guilt.

ALISTAIR. We're simply obeying your husband's orders and he's out looking for a bit of—

JOANNA (quickly). I'll get the sexiest nightie I can find!

(She hurries into the bedroom and exits into dressing room. ALISTAIR reads his note aloud.)

ALISTAIR. "Darling. Go straight to the au pair suite. I'll join you as soon as I'm able to." I'm going to hate myself in the morning.

(As he moves to go the phone rings. He immediately picks up the receiver.)

ALISTAIR (cont.) (on phone, brusquely). Hello ... Miss Smythe? ... staying at Claridges ... written a book. Well done.

(He puts the phone down and dashes out to front door as JOANNA returns with a scarlet nightie and comes through into the living room. ALISTAIR returns immediately.)

ALISTAIR (cont.). I've stuck it on the front—(sees nightie). God help us all.

JOANNA. Don't you like it?

ALISTAIR. Darling, it'll scream with the sheets.

(JOANNA looks back at the sheets and nods.)

JOANNA. I bought it in Spain last year, but never had the courage to wear it.

ALISTAIR. With all those bulls about, very wise.

JOANNA. Well come on. What about your pyjamas?

(She moves into bedroom as ALISTAIR picks up pyjamas and follows her. She stops on seeing the bed and ALISTAIR bumps into her. She drops her nightie and he drops his pyjamas.)

ALISTAIR (losing his courage). I'll change in the study.

(They bend down to pick up their respective nightwear but get the wrong ones. They realise, swop them over, laugh and hurry off—ALISTAIR into study. JOANNA, closing both doors, into dressing room.

WALTER (off). Linda! Lindy-loo!

(After a moment WALTER PANGBOURNE enters diffidently, but grinning hopefully. He is a stiff, slightly vacuous business man. He is wearing a bowler hat and carrying champagne, roses, umbrella and the note. WALTER is between 45 and 50.)

WALTER (cont.) (calling softly). Linda?—Lindy-loo! (He glances down at the note.) "Go straight to the au pair suite." Now I wonder where—

(He looks around and decides to go off into hall U.L. As he exits JOANNA enters from dressing room wearing the nightie under her housecoat. She admires herself in the mirror as WALTER re-enters still looking around. He decides to go off into hall U.R. JOANNA then enters the living room, picks up the champagne and takes it into the bar, half closing the door. SYLVIE enters from the front door, still with her shoulder bag. She looks into the room and is delighted to see ALISTAIR's trousers on the settee. She looks through the open bedroom door and sees the trail of shoes, tie and jacket. She picks up the shoes, then the tie and the jacket on her way into the bedroom and dumps them all together. She opens her shoulder bag and gleefully takes out a very shortie-nightie then happily nips into the dressing room with her nightie, as JOANNA comes out of the bar carrying a tray with the champagne and two glasses. She goes through into the bedroom, shuts the door, puts down the tray, pours herself a drop of champagne, and lies down on top of the bed. During the last part of the previous business WALTER re-enters still looking around and decides that the bedroom must be the au pair suite. He goes to the door and gives a gentle tap. JOANNA takes a quick sip of champagne.)

JOANNA (sweetly). Ready.

54

(WALTER goes into the bedroom, all smiles and kneels beside the bed with one arm outstretched. They look at each other transfixed. After about ten bewildering seconds he politely raises his hat, and hastily retreats from the bedroom. At this moment ALISTAIR enters from the study wearing pyjamas. He and WALTER come face to face and they in turn are transfixed. Once more WALTER raises his hat, takes his visiting card and gives it to ALISTAIR. ALISTAIR looks at it blankly. JOANNA now gets off the bed and hurries into the living room.)

WALTER (to both of them). I can't begin to apologise, frightful gaff. I thought this was the top flat.

JOANNA. It is.

WALTER. Dryden Court.

ALISTAIR. That's right.

WALTER. Oh. I—I didn't expect to find you in, sir.

ALISTAIR. Obviously.

WALTER. Dreadfully embarrassing, Mr. Markham.

ALISTAIR. I'm Mr. Spenlow.

WALTER. Oh.

ALISTAIR. Alistair Spenlow.

WALTER (surprised). Oh. I thought this was the Markhams' flat.

JOANNA. It is.

WALTER. Oh. Well I'm sincerely sorry, Mrs. Spenlow, but—

JOANNA. No—I'm Mrs. Markham.

WALTER. Oh. (Then knowingly.) Ohhhh . . .

JOANNA. You're not Walter!

WALTER. That's right. (Takes another card from his pocket and gives it to JOANNA.) Walter Pangbourne.

JOANNA (reading card). Management Consultant.

ALISTAIR. You haven't managed this very well.

WALTER. When I rang earlier, Mrs. Lodge said that we could—er—here.

JOANNA. Didn't she ring you later to say you couldn't—er—here.

WALTER. No, I put the phone down and rushed round hot-foot.

(The door bell chimes. All three are thrown into a guilty panic. ALISTAIR hastily tries to don his trousers over his pyjamas. WALTER runs round in circles. JOANNA pulls herself together, and goes off to open the door. Both the men rush into the bedroom and shut the door, ALISTAIR having dropped his trousers on the sofa en route. Again they rush about and end up in the bed together with the blanket pulled over their heads. SYLVIE enters from the dressing room in her nightie. She notices the mound on the bed and with joyous anticipation she pulls back the blanket. She is shattered to see ALISTAIR and WALTER with their eyes tight shut cuddling. She immediately puts the blanket back over them and angrily rushes out of the bedroom slamming the door and exits into hall U.R. The men come out of their cuddle on hearing the bedroom door bang and react to each other. WALTER raises his hat again and exits into dressing room. ALISTAIR hides under the blanket again. JOANNA and LINDA enter. LINDA has changed into something "promising" and carries a small vanity case.)

JOANNA. Darling, as far as I know, Henry left some time ago.

LINDA. I tell you, as I was on my way up, I damn near bumped into him.

JOANNA. Henry? Where?

LINDA. He was standing in the main hall. Fortunately he didn't see me.

JOANNA. What on earth's he doing?

LINDA. Up to his old tricks. Bird watching. Scrutinising every girl who walks in. He deserves to get his face slapped.

JOANNA. You deserve to get your bottom slapped. You dropped a page of Walter's letter.

LINDA. No!

JOANNA. Philip thinks it's mine.

LINDA. How sweet of you to take the blame.

JOANNA. He's walked out on me.

LINDA (dramatically). Darling, disaster! (Immediately forgetting it.) Now about my problem—have you seen Walter?

JOANNA. I certainly have. He's about here somewhere, grab him and go.

LINDA. Not likely. If Philip's left, you can pop off to the pictures and we'll make the most of an empty flat. (Goes into bedroom.)

JOANNA (following her into bedroom). Hang on, hold your horses.

LINDA. Surprise, surprise, I'm all yours!

(She whips back the blanket and is somewhat taken aback by the sight of ALISTAIR with his eyes shut and quivering with fear.)

LINDA (cont.). Good God.

ALISTAIR (relieved). Mrs. Lodge.

LINDA. 'Evening, Mr. Spenlow. What are you decorating in there? (Puts her case on the bed.)

JOANNA. He's nothing to do with you.

LINDA (delightedly to JOANNA). Welcome to the club. (Shakes JOANNA's hand.) (To ALISTAIR.) I trust you're enjoying yourself.

ALISTAIR. I would be given half a chance. Everything's so frustrating around here. It's taken me three months to do Mr. Markham's flat and it looks as if I'll be just as long over his wife.

JOANNA. Alistair!

LINDA. Would somebody please tell me, where is Walter?

ALISTAIR. In there.

JOANNA. Just you collect your Speedy Gonzalez and go.

(JOANNA knocks on the door.)

WALTER (off). Who's that?

JOANNA. Room service. Come out.

(WALTER emerges.)

WALTER. Is it safe to—(sees LINDA). Oh Lindy-loo.

LINDA. You mad impetuous boy.

WALTER. Is it on or off?

JOANNA. Off.

(She gives WALTER the case.)

WALTER. What's this?

ALISTAIR. Consolation prize.

WALTER. Can't we stay?

JOANNA. 'Fraid not, there's been a double booking.

WALTER. Well now we're here surely we could come to some arrangement.

LINDA. Like what?

WALTER. Well there's plenty of room for the four of us.

ALISTAIR (jumps out of bed). Good Lord, there's going to be an orgy!

WALTER. What I mean is now we're here, it does seem a frightful waste.

JOANNA. Definitely not. Even at school I lacked the team spirit.

ALISTAIR. Why not try the office?

WALTER. Office?

ALISTAIR. Their suite on the ground floor.

LINDA. Marvellous. Panic over.

WALTER. What about your husband?

LINDA. There's no-one there at this hour and anyway Henry should be delighted. He's always wanted me to do more around the office.

WALTER. Wait a minute. It's probably locked.

LINDA. I've got a key. (To JOANNA.) I see you've sneaked our champagne.

WALTER. Don't worry, precious. I've come prepared. I've got champagne, toothbrush, toothpaste, after shave lotion—

ALISTAIR (hustling him into the living room). Finish the inventory downstairs.

LINDA. Certainly, Alistair. (To JOANNA.) Dear boys, they're both so impatient.

JOANNA. Good night, darling.

ALISTAIR. Cheerio.

WALTER. Au revior, Alistair. (Shakes his hand.)

ALISTAIR. Goodbye, Walter.

WALTER. And once again I do apologise for barging in. I trust you'll be able to carry on from where you—

LINDA (quickly). I'm sure they will.

(LINDA pushes WALTER off. They exit.)

ALISTAIR (after a pause). Well, that's them sorted out. Now, where were we?

JOANNA. Alistair, I think I've gone off the boil.

ALISTAIR. Oh no!

JOANNA. I thought you might be rather relieved.

ALISTAIR. No, initially I was a bit cool, but then I started simmering nicely.

JOANNA. I see.

ALISTAIR (a pause). Are you a long way off the boil?

JOANNA (doubtfully). Well, I think so.

ALISTAIR. I thought you were all for it when your husband said he didn't mind. After all he offered me his pyjamas, his bed and you. Then when he walked out looking for a girl and calling you a floosie—

JOANNA. I'm boiling again! (She strides into the bedroom.)

ALISTAIR. Yoiks!

(JOANNA sits back on the bed and picks up her glass of champagne. At the same time ALISTAIR follows her to the bedroom, merrily. He kicks the door closed and turns the key. On reaching the bed he does a neat little leap and lands beside JOANNA, causing her champagne to shoot into the air and land on her lap. She scrambles off the bed and shakes her housecoat.)

ALISTAIR (cont.). So sorry.

JOANNA. Now I'll have to take it off.

ALISTAIR. Weren't you going to anyway?

(JOANNA goes into the dressing room.)

JOANNA. Yes, but I've got to put it on again, haven't I?

ALISTAIR. Well, it'll dry if we take our time.

(He exits, following her into the dressing room. PHILIP's head appears round the corner of the hallway. He looks round, then tiptoes into the living room. He passes ALISTAIR's trousers on the sofa and then double-takes. He picks them up.)

PHILIP. The swine!

(He throws them down, goes to open the bedroom door and finds it's locked.)

PHILIP (cont.). Double swine!

(He kneels down to look through the keyhole. At that moment SYLVIE enters, still in her nightie. She angrily approaches the bedroom door and then stops on seeing PHILIP crouching there.)

SYLVIE. Oh, Mr. Markham!

PHILIP (straightening up). What the devil—I thought you were out.

SYLVIE. I do not understand what is happening here tonight.

PHILIP. I do and I wish I didn't. What are you doing in your nightie?

SYLVIE (taken aback). Oh. I—er—I was going to bed.

PHILIP. At 8.15?

SYLVIE (fumbling for an excuse). Well, I thought I needed a long lay.

PHILIP. If you wander around like that you'll get one. Go on back to your room.

SYLVIE. Mr. Markham, I do not think you should look in there any more. (Points to the keyhole.)

PHILIP (on his dignity). Go to your room, Sylvie, and allow me to conduct my own affairs.

SYLVIE (determined). Well I think you should know what is going on in there is not very nice.

PHILIP. To put it mildly.

SYLVIE (almost in tears). They are in bed together!

PHILIP. I know!

SYLVIE. Mr. Spenlow is in your pyjamas!

PHILIP. Thank you! Go to your room.

SYLVIE. And the other one is wearing a funny hat.

(She exits.)

PHILIP (amazed). Funny hat?

(ALISTAIR enters bedroom from dressing room carrying a dressing gown and singing "Anchors Aweigh" which very soon develops into just the melody without the words. As soon as PHILIP hears the singing he goes back to the keyhole but by this time ALISTAIR has dropped the dressing gown on the bed, removed his pyjama jacket and hung it on the doorknob—thereby blocking PHILIP's view. PHILIP reacts angrily. While ALISTAIR goes to the mirror and admires himself PHILIP tries to see through the louvres but to no avail.)

ALISTAIR (slapping his chest). You sexy, naked creature.

(PHILIP takes this remark as referring to JOANNA and furiously attempts to see what's going on by looking under the door but again to no avail. ALISTAIR now goes to the bed and decides to test the springs.)

ALISTAIR (cont.) (as he bounces up and down). Wee, Wee, Wee, Wee, Wee.

(PHILIP, unable to see, is now listening in anguish)

ALISTAIR (cont.) (stops bouncing and slaps the bed hard). Well done, my lovely.

(PHILIP, agonised beyond relief, takes a brisk walk to control himself while ALISTAIR looks at his watch and decides to go and see what has happened to JOANNA. He exits to dressing room. PHILIP takes a running kick at the bedroom door, as the front door bell starts to chime. He stops and ricks his back. He hesitates for a moment wondering what to do—he looks from the bedroom door to the hall and decides to hide in the study. He exits to study.)

MISS SMYTHE (calling offstage). Anyone at home—anyone at home.

(MISS SMYTHE enters with briefcase and handbag. She is an imposing "county" lady with a somewhat butterfly mind.

MISS SMYTHE (cont.). Can I come in—? I'm in.

(She walks down and puts her briefcase behind the sofa. She takes a manuscript from it. She starts to glance through the book as SYLVIE tiptoes hurriedly on wearing a short negligee over her nightie. She goes to the bedroom door, listens for a split second, then bangs loudly on the door.)

SYLVIE. Hey!
MISS SMYTHE (jumping). Ahh!

(Her book flies up in the air and the top half dozen pages are scattered. SYLVIE turns, startled. MISS SMYTHE recovers herself.)

SYLVIE. I'm sorry, I did not know there was anyone here, Madam.

MISS SMYTHE. Oh, I'm Miss Smythe. I've called to see Mr. Markham. Are you the girl who "does"?

(SYLVIE looks at the bedroom door, bursts out crying and exits to her room.)

MISS SMYTHE (cont.). Never know where you are with foreigners.

(As she picks up her pages from the floor JOANNA and ALISTAIR enter into the bedroom unheard by MISS SMYTHE in the living room.)

ALISTAIR. I tell you it was the bell. It's probably that damn twit Walter Pangbourne.

JOANNA. Well, hurry up.

ALISTAIR (unlocking the door). Blimey I'll be worn out before we've even started.

(JOANNA goes back into the dressing room. ALISTAIR goes through with his pyjama jacket and dressing gown as SYLVIE enters from hall. They both stop on seeing each other. ALISTAIR goes to her with open arms, SYLVIE stamps on his foot and exits.)

ALISTAIR (cont.). Ow! (He hops off after her.)

MISS SMYTHE (looking up). I beg your pardon?

(She looks round, sees nobody and returns to picking up her pages. Behind her PHILIP comes in stealthily from the study and, without noticing her goes into the bedroom banging door.)

PHILIP. Now what the hell—?! (He stops on seeing bedroom empty.)

MISS SMYTHE (looks up on hearing the door slam). I beg your pardon?

62

(Again she reacts to the fact that the room is empty, then continues collecting her paper.)

JOANNA (off). Alistair!

(PHILIP, on hearing JOANNA's voice nips behind the curtain just as JOANNA enters. As JOANNA continues into living room, PHILIP comes from behind curtain and exits into dressing room. JOANNA moves into hallway to see who was at the front door. By this time MISS SMYTHE has got her book together and seeing JOANNA, moves up behind her. JOANNA turns and comes face to face with MISS SMYTHE. JOANNA looks decidedly puzzled.)

JOANNA (after a pause). Where did you come from?
MISS SMYTHE (after a pause). Norfolk.
JOANNA. Are you the front door bell?

(MISS SMYTHE looks baffled.)

MISS SMYTHE. Are you Mrs. Markham?
JOANNA (considers it). Yes.
MISS SMYTHE. I'm Miss Smythe.
JOANNA. Ah! Ooo! Yes! You telephoned.
MISS SMYTHE. Yes I did.
JOANNA. Twice.
MISS SMYTHE. No, thrice. I want Mr. Markham to read this book I've written.
JOANNA (takes the book). Thank you I'll see you out.

(She ushers MISS SMYTHE to the hall.)

MISS SMYTHE. But I haven't seen Mr. Markham.
JOANNA. Good. Give my regards to Norfolk.
MISS SMYTHE. But I'm in no hurry!
JOANNA. I am. Couldn't you call back tomorrow?
MISS SMYTHE. No I can't come back tomorrow. I shall be in Norfolk with my darling little doggie woggies. I want Mr. Markham to give me a decision on my book tonight.
JOANNA. Out of the question.
MISS SMYTHE. I thought it would be quite easy for the authoress of the Bow-Wow Books, considering their popularity.

JOANNA (chuckling politely). The Bow-Wow Books. Yes, well, of course, if you were an Olive Harriet—(suddenly realises) Smythe!! (She looks at the book and reads the title) "The Further Adventures of Bow-Wow and Little Woofer. By Olive Harriet Smythe."

MISS SMYTHE. That's me.

JOANNA. But surely you already have a publisher.

MISS SMYTHE. I did until yesterday. Then we had a serious disagreement. I discovered they had printed an obscene book—Filthy—I read it twice. So now I'm looking for a new publisher.

JOANNA (agog). For all your future Bow-Wow Books?

MISS SMYTHE. Yes.

JOANNA (gushing over her). My dear Miss Smythe, do come in, do sit down.

(She rushes MISS SMYTHE into a seat.)

MISS SMYTHE. I've come to your firm because I've heard you don't go in for sex.

JOANNA. Quite right.

MISS SMYTHE. There's no need for it is there? Do you know my last publisher made a million out of my Bow-Wows.

JOANNA. You've definitely come to the right firm.

(She dashes to the phone and picks up the receiver.)

MISS SMYTHE. Who are you phoning?

JOANNA. I don't know. I'll think of someone. I'll ring Mr. Lodge's house and leave a message for him.

MISS SMYTHE. I do have a train to catch. Isn't your husband at home?

(ALISTAIR returns from the hall.)

ALISTAIR. I don't know what's going on round here—I really don't. I didn't even get to the front door—Good evening.

(He stops on seeing MISS SMYTHE. MISS SMYTHE looks at him in his dressing gown and pyjamas.)

JOANNA (putting down the receiver). Hullo, darling!

MISS SMYTHE. Ah, you must be Mr. Markham.

ALISTAIR. Must I?

JOANNA (to ALISTAIR). Yes you must. Darling this is Miss *Smythe*. Miss *Olive Smythe*. Miss *Olive Harriet Smythe*.

MISS SMYTHE. That's me.

JOANNA (to ALISTAIR pointedly). And Miss Smythe is considering giving you all her Bow-Wows.

(ALISTAIR looks around to see where they are.)

MISS SMYTHE. I dare say that surprises you.

ALISTAIR. Yes.

JOANNA (handing ALISTAIR the book). For you!

ALISTAIR (taking it blankly). Thank you. (Reads.) "The Further Adventures of Bow-Wow and Little Woofer."

(He closes his eyes in anguish.)

MISS SMYTHE (to JOANNA). He's obviously quite overcome.

JOANNA. He'll get over it. (To ALISTAIR.) You go and change. Get out of your pyjamas, darling, then we can have a nice chat to Miss Smythe about her book.

MISS SMYTHE. I'm all in favour of wearing clothes to suit the climate. Pyjamas, most suitable for these warm evenings. It's quite balmy out.

ALISTAIR. It's not too good in here.

MISS SMYTHE. I'm sorry to barge in like this but you did promise to ring me back.

JOANNA. Why didn't you ring back, darling?

ALISTAIR (pointedly). Because I was going to bed, darling.

MISS SMYTHE. Bed? It's very early.

JOANNA (to ALISTAIR, laughing). Darling!

MISS SMYTHE. Is he a little queer?

ALISTAIR. No, he's not!

MISS SMYTHE. Oh, good. Well now, I'd like you to read my book tonight, if possible.

ALISTAIR. It isn't. I'm hoping to have a go at "Goldilocks".

(He looks pointedly at JOANNA who once more laughs gaily.)

JOANNA. I think it might be better, Miss Smythe, if you were to wait in the study while my husband gets dressed.

MISS SMYTHE. I don't leave my doggie woggies longer than necessary. So I must settle this publisher business before I go back to the country. I've got eighteen Cockers and a Boxer. I try to be impartial but the Boxer is my favourite. Great sloppy thing. Have you ever been kissed by a Boxer?

ALISTAIR. Not recently. No.

MISS SMYTHE (to JOANNA). Although they're extremely well cared for in my absence. (Turns to ALISTAIR.) Did I tell you I have a man who "does"?

ALISTAIR. No.

MISS SMYTHE. Charming man, salt of the earth. Now what's his name, he hasn't done for me long. Thomas something or something Thomas. Oh it's a dreadful nuisance—not my man who does—publishers in general—no offence.

JOANNA. None taken.

MISS SMYTHE. That's why I want a new publisher. There's too much sex around these days. That's why we're all going down hill fast. All this stripping and showing their nudal frontities—disgusting. And what I object to is being hit in the face with it.

JOANNA. Yes.

MISS SMYTHE. That's what I told my publisher. (Suddenly.) Thompson! He's not my publisher. He's my man who does me.

(ALISTAIR and JOANNA look startled.)

MISS SMYTHE (cont.). So I want to find out if Mr. Markham is interested in my Bow-Wow Books.

JOANNA. Just give him a few minutes to change. He really mustn't mix business with pyjamas.

MISS SMYTHE. Yes. Yes. I think I'd feel easier if he took them off. Oh, what have I said?

JOANNA. Won't keep you a moment.

(JOANNA shows MISS SMYTHE into the study.)

ALISTAIR. What's she on about?

JOANNA. About half a million a year. Miss Smythe and her Bow Wow Books are the hottest thing since Mickey Mouse.

ALISTAIR. Gawd help us all.

JOANNA (pushing him towards bedroom). Go in there and get dressed while I think of some way to deal with the situation.

(MISS SMYTHE re-enters from study.)

MISS SMYTHE. Jackson!

JOANNA. I beg your pardon?

MISS SMYTHE. Jackson is my present gardener. Thompson did me years ago. I'm afraid one of my dogs bit him so, of course, we had to have him put down.

(She exits to study.)

JOANNA (to ALISTAIR). Hurry up while I think how to deal with Miss Smythe.

(She picks up his trousers and pushes him to bedroom door as PHILIP comes out of dressing room door. On hearing their approaching voices he steps into the recess behind the curtain.)

ALISTAIR. Does that mean our game's been abandoned?

JOANNA. We'll inspect the pitch later. Get in there.

(She opens bedroom door, pushes him in and follows.)

ALISTAIR. Everything happens so quickly round here.

JOANNA. Don't talk, just get your pyjamas off and do what I tell you to do.

(JOANNA starts to undo ALISTAIR's jacket.)

ALISTAIR (giggles). Stop it, you're tickling. I'll only make a fool of myself.

JOANNA. No you won't. Over the years I've learned quite a lot from Philip.

(PHILIP seething with anger, flings the curtains aside.)

PHILIP (as he does so). Ahhh!

(JOANNA spins round and ALISTAIR, in one movement, turns and somersaults on to the bed.)

JOANNA (to PHILIP). Darling, I've had the most
wonderful surprise.
PHILIP. Have you?
ALISTAIR. I think I'll just toddle along.
PHILIP. Shut up!

(ALISTAIR freezes.)

JOANNA. Philip there's someone—
PHILIP (pressing on). I'm absolutely appalled at what I've
seen here tonight.
JOANNA. What have you seen?
PHILIP. Nothing, that's what so damn crafty. You hung
something over the keyhole, didn't you?
ALISTAIR. Oh, been at the keyhole again, have you?
PHILIP. Shut up!

(ALISTAIR freezes again.)

PHILIP (cont.). You might have stopped me seeing but I
heard plenty.
JOANNA. Oh you stupid oaf!
PHILIP. Yes! Yes, you're right, quite right. I am stupid to
have given the best years of my life to a strumpet.
JOANNA (blandly). Anyone we know?
PHILIP. Don't try to be witty with me. Keep it for your
pouffy paperhanger.
ALISTAIR. If you call me that once more. (Raising his fist
to PHILIP.)
JOANNA (restrains him). Alistair! There are more
important—
ALISTAIR. If anyone's pouffy round here, it's him, he's as
queer as a coot.
JOANNA. How dare you. Philip and I have been married
for fif— (she stops). You're not, are you, Philip?
PHILIP. Of course I'm not.
JOANNA. Of course he's not. For heaven's sake. He plays
golf.
PHILIP. And don't change the subject. We're discussing
your despicable behaviour this evening and that filthy love
letter you wrote to my wife.

ALISTAIR. Not only pouffy, but potty.

JOANNA. Philip, darling, it wasn't from him and it wasn't to me. I've been utterly faithful.

PHILIP. So why were you undressing him just now?

ALISTAIR (stepping down off the bed). I'm glad you asked—

PHILIP. Shut up!

(ALISTAIR leaps back on to the bed.)

PHILIP (cont.) (to JOANNA). And why are *you* undressed if you weren't going to bed with him?

JOANNA. Because I *was* going to bed with him!

PHILIP. I knew it. Abandoned sex!

JOANNA. *You* abandoned it ages ago.

PHILIP. Me?! You're always asleep before I've got my socks off.

JOANNA. Why the hell don't you check to see if I'm asleep?!

PHILIP. Because I thought you'd lost interest!

JOANNA. Well, I haven't!

PHILIP (suddenly tender). Oh, my little Jo-Jo.

ALISTAIR. Oh, blimey.

PHILIP (rounding on him). You've got a nerve flaunting your torso in front of my Jo-Jo.

JOANNA. He was getting ready for Miss Smythe in the study.

PHILIP. Is he trying to establish a record?

JOANNA. The Miss Smythe who telephoned is Olive Harriet Smythe.

PHILIP (pole-axed). Olive Harriet Smythe.

JOANNA. Her old publishers have gone in for pornography, so she wants you to handle all the future Bow-Wow Books.

PHILIP (agog). She what?

JOANNA. Starting with "The Further Adventures of Bow-Wow and Little Woofer."

PHILIP (shaking with excitement). The Bow-Wow Books! She wants me to publish the—it'll put us right up there with "Hodder and Stoughton". (Turns excitedly to ALISTAIR.) Did you hear that, she wants us to publish the Bow-Wow Books. Peter Pooch, Big Woofer, Little Woofer.

ALISTAIR. Shut up!

PHILIP (to JOANNA). Darling, you're wonderful. (He gives

her a quick peck, then glances at ALISTAIR.) I'll deal with you later. Right now, I'm going to meet Miss Smythe.

JOANNA (grabbing his arm). You can't.

PHILIP. Why not?

JOANNA. You've already met her.

PHILIP. I've what?

JOANNA. She thinks Alistair's you!

PHILIP. Alistair!?

JOANNA. Yes. Alistair's got to chat to Miss Smythe about the contract.

PHILIP. I'm not having an important contract negotiated by the builder.

ALISTAIR. Builder!

(He goes into the living room followed by JOANNA and ALISTAIR.)

JOANNA. Well *you* can't do it.

PHILIP. No, I know. I'm going to find Henry.

JOANNA. Do you know where he is?

PHILIP. Yes. He's standing on the corner watching all the girls go by.

(He exits as the study door opens and MISS SMYTHE emerges.)

MISS SMYTHE. Look, I really must explain. The dog was put down, not the gardener. You're still in your pyjamas.

ALISTAIR. Yes, I am.

JOANNA. I'm awfully sorry about that but I'm having some difficulty in persuading him to get dressed.

(She moves her back to study.)

MISS SMYTHE (stopping and moving to ALISTAIR). But surely this is important business.

JOANNA. So important in fact that my husband's sent for his partner, Mr. Lodge.

MISS SMYTHE. Why can't Mr. Markham deal with it. (She looks at ALISTAIR.)

ALISTAIR. Well, you know how it is.

MISS SMYTHE. How what is?

ALISTAIR. Well, I—you—she—we—

JOANNA (quickly). We're on our honeymoon.

MISS SMYTHE (delighted). Honeymoon?

ALISTAIR. Oh Gawd.

MISS SMYTHE. And when was the wedding?

JOANNA. What wedding? Oh! This morning.

MISS SMYTHE (to JOANNA). Congratulations. (Rushing to ALISTAIR.) Gratters! Gratters!

ALISTAIR. Thank you.

MISS SMYTHE. You never told me.

ALISTAIR. You never asked.

MISS SMYTHE. Oh you are a naughty boy. No wonder you're in your—(she chuckles). Perhaps I'd *better* see Mr. Lodge.

JOANNA. If you could just wait in the study.

MISS SMYTHE. Certainly. I'm not married myself but I do adore weddings. Always the bridesmaid, that's me.

ALISTAIR. Me too.

(The intercom buzzes.)

MISS SMYTHE. What was that?

JOANNA (flustered.) The office, downstairs.

(The intercom buzzes the S.O.S. signal urgently three times. JOANNA is nonplussed for a second.)

MISS SMYTHE. Shall I answer it.

JOANNA (to ALISTAIR). It'll be for you, darling. I'll take Miss Smythe back into the study.

MISS SMYTHE. I hope Mr. Lodge won't be too long. I've got a little problem with my train.

JOANNA. We'll find you something else to play with.

(She hustles MISS SMYTHE into the study. The buzzer goes and ALISTAIR answers it.)

ALISTAIR (irritably). Hullo ... Oh Walter ... No you haven't interrupted anything ... office teapot? What d'you want that for, you've got champagne down there ... (flatly) she says she can't do anything until she's had a cup of tea, well hard luck ... No, Mrs. Markham's busy, and I don't know where they keep anything. Tell her to get steamed up on a glass of water.

(As he replaces the receiver SYLVIE enters from
hallway. She is now dressed again and angrily makes
straight for the bedroom. ALISTAIR sees her.)

ALISTAIR (cont.). Darling!
SYLVIE. Oh, there you are. I may as well tell you I saw
you in bed with that "other person".
ALISTAIR. Oh, hell! It wasn't all that serious.
SYLVIE. Not serious?
ALISTAIR. Just a bit of 'How's-your-Father".
SYLVIE (looking towards bedroom). Your father?
ALISTAIR. When someone as pretty as that offers themself
to you you've just got to—
SYLVIE. Oh!

(SYLVIE storms out, back to her room.)

ALISTAIR. Sylvie, listen.

(He starts to follow her and the telephone rings. He
grabs it up and answers it.)

ALISTAIR (cont.). Hullo . . . No this is not Mr. Markham.
Who wants him? Beau who? . . . Street? Oh, Bow Street . . .
Mr. Lodge is being held for questioning? What for? . . . Oo, I
see! (Chuckling.) Very good! (He puts the phone down.)

(PHILIP hurries in from hallway.)

PHILIP. I can't find Henry anywhere.
ALISTAIR. No, he wants you to bail him out.
PHILIP. Right, I'll go—bail him out!?
ALISTAIR. Well, vouch for him or something. He's been
pulled in to Bow Street.
PHILIP. What for?
ALISTAIR. Soliciting.

(He exits.)

PHILIP. Oh no.

(JOANNA hurries out of the study and closes the door.)

JOANNA. Have you managed to grab Henry?

PHILIP. No, I was beaten to it.

JOANNA. How long's he going to be?

PHILIP. About twenty-eight days I should think.

(He hurries into the bedroom.)

JOANNA (following him). Twenty-eight days? What's he up to?

PHILIP (indicates his chin). Here. (Picks up the telephone directory to look up "Police".) I'd better ring Bow Street. They want me to vouch for him.

JOANNA. Miss Smythe is in the study and she's more important than Henry, and she's getting impatient.

PHILIP. Stay with her in the study while I sort this out. Then I'll talk to her.

JOANNA. You *can't* talk to her. She thinks Alistair's you.

PHILIP. Alright then, I'll have to be Henry.

JOANNA. But you don't know enough about his side of the business. You only read the books.

PHILIP. Now's my chance to learn. You keep Miss Smythe chatting.

JOANNA. I can't stop her. I've heard all about the Woofer family from Grandad Growl to Baby Yappy.

MISS SMYTHE (off). Mrs. Markham!

(JOANNA hurries back towards the study closing the bedroom door, with PHILIP still looking for the number. The study door opens and MISS SMYTHE enters.)

MISS SMYTHE. Any sign of Mr. Lodge yet?

JOANNA. Yes, he's on his way.

MISS SMYTHE. Oh, good. Because I can't let you keep me talking here all evening. I was telling you about the Woofers, wasn't I? In this latest book you'll be interested to learn that they've moved from the Isle of Dogs.

JOANNA (moving MISS SMYTHE back). What a wise decision.

MISS SMYTHE. Can you guess where they're living now?

JOANNA. Houndsditch.

MISS SMYTHE (chortles merrily then stops). No. Barking.

(They go off into the study and PHILIP, who has been unable to find the number, starts to diall 100 as MISS

WILKINSON enters. She is a 27-year-old ex-deb, very
pretty, kooky, with large horn-rimmed glasses. She looks
around enquiringly and comes into the living room.)

MISS WILKINSON (calling softly). Mr. Lodge? It's me,
Miss Wilkinson.

(She looks round the room and is obviously impressed.)

MISS WILKINSON (cont.). Mr. Lodge?
PHILIP (on phone). Hullo, operator. Hullo, operator.

(MISS WILKINSON comes through the door.)

MISS WILKINSON. Hullo.
PHILIP. Hullo. Oh! (Taking her for MISS SMYTHE.) I
thought you were still chatting in the—er—with my—er—(puts
phone down). I'm terribly sorry, you must be getting
impatient.
MISS WILKINSON (slightly taken aback). No.
PHILIP. Well, I'll just tell you very briefly my normal terms
of agreement.
MISS WILKINSON. It *is* Mr. Lodge, isn't it?
PHILIP. Er—well—(decides to take the plunge). Of course,
who else? Henry Lodge Esq., Senior partner of Lodge and
Markham and I can't tell you how thrilled I am at the prospect
of handling you.

(There is a pause as MISS WILKINSON considers the
startling rapidity of this approach.)

MISS WILKINSON (quite impressed). You don't hang
about, do you?
PHILIP. No. I must say you're far younger than I expected.
MISS WILKINSON (non-plussed). Thank you.
PHILIP. Now shall we get down to it right away.
MISS WILKINSON. Honestly! I thought we'd at least have
time to get to know each other—you know, a chat and a drink.
PHILIP. Well, if you must, but a very quick one, and not
too much chat.

(He pours out two glasses of champagne using the glasses
and champagne brought in by JOANNA earlier.)

PHILIP (cont.). Now, one thing we ought to get straight before we start. How long are you prepared to be tied down?

MISS WILKINSON. What does that mean?

PHILIP. Initially I'd like you to agree to three years.

MISS WILKINSON. Three years?

PHILIP (hastily). But I'd always let you go after six months if you're not completely satisfied. Cheers!

MISS WILKINSON. Cheers! Do you have a lot of success with this direct approach?

PHILIP (confidingly). Well, to be absolutely honest, tonight's the first time I've done it.

MISS WILKINSON (surprised). Ever?

PHILIP (nods). Yes.

MISS WILKINSON (gently). Ahh.

PHILIP. What I mean is that I'm generally the one who just reads the books.

MISS WILKINSON (more gently). Ahh.

PHILIP. But I can promise one thing, you'll be treated with the utmost courtesy. Please say "yes". It would mean so much to me.

MISS WILKINSON. Oh, what the hell. O.K. (Hands him her glass.)

PHILIP. Wonderful, wonderful. I'm only sorry it's so rushed this evening.

(He takes her glass and puts it, and his, on the dressing table. As he turns away MISS WILKINSON, in one quick movement, unzips her dress and steps out of it.)

PHILIP (cont.). I assure you, you'll have my constant and devoted attention. It's really just a matter of drawing up a simple—

(He turns and stops dead in his tracks. MISS WILKINSON lays her dress down, slips her shoes off and gets into bed. For about ten seconds PHILIP's mind whirls.)

PHILIP (cont.) (finally). Aren't you feeling well?

MISS WILKINSON. Fine.

(MISS WILKINSON removes her bra under the bedclothes and drops it on the floor. PHILIP stands

(there, his face blank as he surveys her. She pulls the bedclothes to her chin and struggles out of her panties which she also drops on the floor.)

PHILIP. Just tired perhaps.

MISS WILKINSON. Now, look, if you're short of time you better strip off and hop in. (She pats the bed.)

PHILIP. Could we just stick to books?

MISS WILKINSON. I thought you wanted to go a stage further.

PHILIP. Well, I don't. I mean I never dreamed that you er—what I'm trying to say is that I only want to talk about your Little Woofer.

MISS WILKINSON. My what?!

(HENRY enters from the hallway looking distraught. As PHILIP waffles on, HENRY strides into the room and stands right behind PHILIP.)

PHILIP. And when we have more time there's plenty still to discuss. We've got to go into the question of options, foriegn rights—and how you feel about having it illustrated.

(MISS WILKINSON stares at him blankly. By this time HENRY is standing beside him.)

PHILIP (cont.). And if you're agreeable, I'd like to see your "Bow-Wow" fully exploited. Can you imagine all the cornflake packets carrying pictures of your "Woofers"?

HENRY. Philip!

(PHILIP jumps out of his skin.)

HENRY (cont.) (to MISS WILKINSON). I'm sorry to interrupt whatever's going on, but I have something to say to my partner.

(PHILIP picks up the dress, bra and pants as he talks.)

PHILIP. Nothing's going on at all. We were just discussing terms of agreement. This is Miss Smythe.

HENRY. Smythe?

MISS WILKINSON. Smythe?

PHILIP. Olive Harriet Smythe.

HENRY. You're not Olive Harriet Smythe?

MISS WILKINSON. No. Felicity Jane Wilkinson.

HENRY. Wilkinson!?

PHILIP. Wilkinson?

(HENRY slowly looks round at PHILIP as the implication dawns on him.)

PHILIP (cont.). I think I've made a couple of teensy-weensy mistakes. First of all, madam, may I introduce Mr. Lodge.

MISS WILKINSON. You said *you* were Mr. Lodge.

PHILIP. That was my first mistake. You see I took Miss Wilkinson—

HENRY (quickly). And that was your second.

MISS WILKINSON (to HENRY). Well if you're Mr. Lodge, who's this?

HENRY. My partner. My *junior* partner.

PHILIP. We were going to to discuss this book, you see.

HENRY. The Kama Sutra?

PHILIP. No, the Bow-Wow Books.

HENRY. The Bow-Wow Books?

PHILIP. Miss Smythe is here, and if we can sign her up we're going to publish them.

HENRY. Well done. You deal with Miss Smythe, I'll deal with Miss Wilkinson.

PHILIP. No. Don't you realise we've got Grandad Growl? Baby Yappy? Peter Pooch? All the Woofer family?

MISS WILKINSON. What *is* this? Battersea Dogs' Home?

HENRY. I do apologise, but Mr. Markham, for once in his life, has excelled himself.

PHILIP. Henry, you clinch this and our future is assured.

MISS WILKINSON. Well, I can't see much future for me so would you mind leaving the room while I get dressed.

(She stands up on the bed with the sheet in front of her.)

PHILIP. Good idea.

HENRY. No, please. My dear Miss Wilkinson, I haven't yet had the chance to tell you how absolutely ravishing you look. You're just as I pictured you.

PHILIP. First things first. Can't you imagine what it'll be like if you pull it off.

HENRY (eyeing MISS WILKINSON). I'm working on it.

(JOANNA comes out of the study and calls urgently.)

JOANNA. Philip!

MISS WILKINSON (scared). Who's that?

HENRY (equally scared). His wife.

PHILIP. I'll introduce you.

HENRY (stops him). No you won't.

PHILIP. No I won't.

JOANNA (goes to the hallway). Darling?

(HENRY bundles the naked MISS WILKINSON up in a sheet, and pushes her through the dressing room door. At the same time PHILIP stuffs the dress, bra and pants inside his jacket and makes for the living room door to forestall JOANNA's entrance.)

JOANNA (cont.). Phi—

PHILIP (entering and shutting door behind him). What d'you want? What d'you want?

JOANNA. You or Henry.

PHILIP. What for? What for?

JOANNA. Well, what are you doing about this wretched woman and her Woofers.

PHILIP. Never touched 'em. Never touched 'em. (Realising). Oh Miss—er—yes.

(HENRY re-enters from the dressing room and hurries into the living room.)

JOANNA. Have you sorted out Henry's problem?

PHILIP. Never touched 'em.

(HENRY enters.)

JOANNA. What on earth's the matter—(sees HENRY.) I thought you'd been arrested.

HENRY. They realised they had to let me go.

JOANNA. That was lucky.

HENRY. And expensive.

PHILIP. Don't tell me you gave them another two bob.

HENRY. It cost me twelve pounds in raffle tickets. (He takes out a wad of raffle books and gives them to PHILIP.) The draw's being made at the Annual Police Ball. That's on July 31st. I've got tickets for that too. (Gives them to JOANNA.)

JOANNA. What about Miss Smythe?

PHILIP. Yes, what about her?

HENRY. Why not, it says "and guest".

JOANNA. I'll tell her you're here, Henry.

(She goes quickly into the study.)

PHILIP. What have you done with that girl of yours?

HENRY. Don't worry, she'll keep, she's in the airing cupboard.

PHILIP. Oh dear. Get rid of her.

HENRY. After you've done such a masterful job of preparation?

PHILIP. That was an accident.

HENRY. Heaven help her if you'd really been trying.

PHILIP. You've got to deal with Olive Harriet Smythe.

HENRY. As a matter of interest, why's she left her old publisher?

PHILIP. He was getting a bit too involved with sex.

HENRY (glances towards the bedroom.) Bloody 'ell.

PHILIP. Quite. So remove Miss Wilkinson first.

HENRY. Safer to remove Miss Smythe. I'll get her signature on one of our letter contracts right away.

PHILIP. Good idea. Nip down to the office and get one.

HENRY. The office, right.

(He exits. PHILIP takes out bra, pants and dress and starts to tip-toe towards the bedroom door.)

JOANNA (off). After you, Miss Smythe.

(As the study door opens PHILIP steps neatly into the bar and shuts the door. JOANNA and MISS SMYTHE enter from study.)

MISS SMYTHE. It's very, very difficult, Mrs. Markham, you know my main worry is what to do with myself in the mating season.

JOANNA (opening bedroom door). Henry—

MISS SMYTHE. You haven't lost those men again, have you?

JOANNA. Hmmm? No.

    (ALISTAIR enters from the hallway not seeing MISS SMYTHE.)

ALISTAIR (to JOANNA). I'm off now.

JOANNA. Off?!

ALISTAIR. I'm taking Sylvie out.

MISS SMYTHE. Taking Sylvie out?

JOANNA (quickly). No, darling. *Philip, Philip* darling. (Then gaily to MISS SMYTHE.) He wants to take Sylvie out. That's our au pair girl. He's so good to her. (To ALISTAIR.) You've forgotten, Philip, she's out already. You and Mr. Lodge must stay here, sign up Miss Smythe, then Miss Smythe can catch her train back to Norfolk and we can all live happily ever after.

MISS SMYTHE. I like your turn of phrase, Mrs. Markham.

ALISTAIR. I'll leave it all to Mr. Lodge, I've got better things to do tonight.

JOANNA. Darling. (To MISS SMYTHE.) You must forgive Alistair.

MISS SMYTHE. Yes of course—(then puzzled.) Alistair?

    (JOANNA and ALISTAIR look at each other.)

JOANNA. Yes—Alistair—that's our dog.

MISS SMYTHE (delighted). You never told me you had a doggie woggie!

ALISTAIR. Here we go again.

MISS SMYTHE. Where is he? Let Alistair meet his Auntie Olive.

JOANNA. He's not very well today.

MISS SMYTHE. Oh dear.

JOANNA. He's usually here to greet people, but we won't disturb him now. He's in his basket with a hot nose. (She indicates the bedroom.)

MISS SMYTHE. Poor little pooch.

JOANNA. He might rally later on. In the meantime do have a drink.

MISS SMYTHE. Well, I don't usually. It's the same as sex, isn't it?

JOANNA. No.

MISS SMYTHE. If it's taken to excess, I mean. One of my uncles died of it—drink, I mean, not the other thing.

JOANNA. Yes.

MISS SMYTHE. And you should have seen what it did to one of my men who did, who did. But perhaps just a small one to celebrate the deal. Not to mention your honeymoon. (She chuckles.)

JOANNA. Yes. Darling, fix us all a drink.

ALISTAIR. I think I could do with one.

(He goes towards the bar.)

JOANNA (to MISS SMYTHE). What would you like?

MISS SMYTHE. What have you got in there, Mr. Markham?

ALISTAIR. You name it, we've got it.

(He slides the door open and comes face to face with PHILIP who is standing there with his jacket off and a tea towel tucked into his trousers as an apron. He does his best to look like a butler when he remembers it.)

JOANNA (after a pause). What the dickens are you doing in there?

PHILIP. Coming out, madam.

(He does so and tries to adopt a butler's walk.)

JOANNA (to PHILIP). I thought I gave you the night off.

PHILIP. So you did, Madam, but I remembered I'd left behind a couple of dirty dishes.

(JOANNA and ALISTAIR react to this.)

MISS SMYTHE. Oh, is this your man who does?

(JOANNA and PHILIP look at each other.)

JOANNA. This is our butler.

PHILIP (to MISS SMYTHE). Good evening, madam. (To JOANNA.) Good evening, madam.

(He turns to come face to face with ALISTAIR.)

PHILIP (cont.) (coldly to ALISTAIR). Good evening, sir.

JOANNA (to ALISTAIR). Order something, darling.

ALISTAIR. Oh, yes er—

PHILIP (gritting his teeth). What'll it be, "sir"?

ALISTAIR. Well, we'd all like a drink please Mr. Mar—Mar—martini for me. And how about you, Mrs. Mar—Mar—dar—dar—ling.

JOANNA. Gin and bitter lemon please, darling.

ALISTAIR. Jolly good darling. (To PHILIP.) Have you got that?

PHILIP. Yes, sir. One martini, one gin and "bitter" lemon.

ALISTAIR. That's right. (To MISS SMYTHE.) What about you, darling? I mean Miss—Miss—

MISS SMYTHE. Smythe.

ALISTAIR. Smythe.

MISS SMYTHE. Sherry

ALISTAIR. Sherry.

PHILIP. A votre service.

(PHILIP exits into bar once more adopting his butler's walk. JOANNA raises her eyes to heaven.)

MISS SMYTHE. He seems quite personable.

ALISTAIR. Bloody insolent if you ask me.

JOANNA. Language, dear, language.

MISS SMYTHE. It's quite alright, Mr. Markham, I think I can understand his irritability. He's anxious to get you back into bed again!

(There is a loud crash from the bar.)

JOANNA (light-heartedly). Whoops.

(The bar door slides open revealing PHILIP.)

JOANNA. Any damage?

PHILIP (putting his head out. Flatly). Broken a quantity of glasses.

(He disappears again closing door.)

MISS SMYTHE. While we're waiting for Mr. Lodge—

JOANNA. Yes, I'm sorry, I don't know where Henry's got to.

MISS SMYTHE (to ALISTAIR). Well in the meantime perhaps you could tell me the usual sort of agreement you have with your clients.

ALISTAIR. I deduct 20% if they buy their own paper.

(JOANNA tries to indicate to ALISTAIR that he's put his foot in it.)

MISS SMYTHE. I beg your pardon?

JOANNA (gaily). Don't be flippant, darling. (To MISS SMYTHE.) From the odd remark that Philip drops I gather for one thing that the publisher gets a percentage of your royalties.

MISS SMYTHE. Yes. In the past I've paid ten per cent.

ALISTAIR. You were robbed. We'll do it for five.

JOANNA (hastily). No! I think Philip should be here.

MISS SMYTHE (indicates ALISTAIR). Well he *is* here.

JOANNA. Oh Philip, yes. No, what I said was I think Phil*ips* should be here.

MISS SMYTHE. Who?

JOANNA. Phil*ips.* That's our butler. Phil*ips.*

MISS SMYTHE (to ALISTAIR). Don't you find that confusing?

ALISTAIR. Very.

MISS SMYTHE. I can't quite see that this has anything to do with your butler.

JOANNA. That's what you think. (Calls out.) Philips!

PHILIP (appearing). Yes, madam?

JOANNA. I'll finish the drinks. I think it would be a good idea if you attend to Miss Smythe.

PHILIP. I'd much rather attend to Mr. Markham.

JOANNA. So devoted.

(She exits into bar closing door.)

ALISTAIR (enjoying himself). It's quite alright, Philips, I'm just going to cut our commission down by half.

PHILIP. Oh no you won't! (Then smiling to MISS SMYTHE.) If I may be so bold. (To ALISTAIR.) Why not wait until your partner, Mr. Lodge, returns with the contract.

ALISTAIR. That's not necessary.

PHILIP. Oh yes it is! (He then quickly smiles to MISS SMYTHE.) If I may be so bold.

MISS SMYTHE (to ALISTAIR). Your Mr. Lodge seems to be somewhat elusive.

ALISTAIR. Yes.

PHILIP. If I may be so bold—

MISS SMYTHE. Oh dear, what is it now?

PHILIP. I happen to know the precise wherabouts of the afore-mentioned Mr. Lodge.

MISS SMYTHE. Do you? Splendid.

PHILIP. He's just gone down to get the contract from the office.

(There is another loud glass crash from the bar. Everyone looks as JOANNA appears.)

PHILIP (cont.). What the hell have you done?

JOANNA (nervously). Nothing, just broken some glasses.

PHILIP. You clumsy idiot!

MISS SMYTHE (shocked). Steady, Philips.

PHILIP. If I may be so bold.

JOANNA (firmly). Just get the drinks.

(She pushes him into the bar and closes the door. She then rushes to the intercom phone and buzzes.)

MISS SMYTHE. Anything the matter, Mrs. Markham?

JOANNA (buzzing furiously). No, nothing. (To herself.) Come on, come on.

MISS SMYTHE. Thought maybe you were ordering some more glasses.

(HENRY enters from the hallway not expecting to find anyone but PHILIP.)

HENRY. Damn funny the office is locked.

JOANNA (slams the phone down). Henry! Darling, where *have* you been?

HENRY. Trying to get into the office, it's locked on the inside. At first I thought it must be someone doing a bit of overtime.

JOANNA. Oh. And was it?

HENRY. No. I banged, but no answer.

JOANNA. Never mind, now you're here let me introduce you to Miss Smythe.

HENRY (ecstatically). My dear lady.

MISS SMYTHE. The elusive Mr. Lodge, I presume. Have I caught you on a busy night?

HENRY. Very nearly. (Quickly.) But as soon as I heard you'd arrived I dropped everything.

MISS SMYTHE. Thank you.

JOANNA (pointedly). And of course Philip is here.

HENRY. Yes I know, where?

ALISTAIR (helpfully). Hullo, Henry old man.

HENRY (blankly). Huh?

ALISTAIR (patting him on the back). Didn't expect to find me sorting things out, did you?

HENRY. No, I didn't.

ALISTAIR. You know me, your old "cream paint mahogany loving" partner.

HENRY (lost). What's wrong with Alistair?

MISS SMYTHE. Don't worry he's got worms.

HENRY. Worms?

MISS SMYTHE. They're about a lot these days.

(PHILIP comes out of the bar.)

PHILIP. Did you say Mar—Henry!—Mr. Lodge, *sir*.

HENRY. Hmmm?

JOANNA (quickly). You've seen Philips, haven't you?

HENRY. Philip's what?

PHILIP. No, sir, begging your pardon, sir. We did meet earlier, sir. I'm Phil*ips*. The butler.

HENRY. Butler?

MISS SMYTHE. Butler.

JOANNA. The new butler.

HENRY. The new—

MISS SMYTHE. Butler.

PHILIP. Are you with us now, sir?

MISS SMYTHE. Well, are you with us?

HENRY. Just about—and Alistair's got worms.

MISS SMYTHE. Yes. Or distemper.

HENRY (lost again). Distemper?

JOANNA. He's never been a healthy *dog*, you know that, Henry.

HENRY. Ah, *dog*. Now lets hang on to that. Refresh my memory, what type of dog is Alistair?

PHILIP. Dirty.

JOANNA. No, no, he's er—

ALISTAIR. Er—

JOANNA ⎫ Together. Labrador.
ALISTAIR ⎭ Poodle.

JOANNA ⎫ Together. Poodle.
ALISTAIR ⎭ Labrador.

JOANNA. Half and half.

PHILIP (sarcastically). Very rare, labradoodles. Think I'll have a whisky.

ALISTAIR. Not while you're on duty, Philips.

(PHILIP stops in his tracks and glares at ALISTAIR.)

MISS SMYTHE. Do you know I've never come across a labradoodle.

PHILIP. As I said, madam, very rare.

MISS SMYTHE. I can't imagine what that kind of cross-breed would look like.

HENRY (looking at ALISTAIR). Nine inches tall, four foot long and minces about with a bow in its hair.

JOANNA. I'm sure Miss Smythe would like to settle the question of the contract.

HENRY. Yes. (Looking at PHILIP.)

MISS SMYTHE. Yes, time's getting on, and my doggie woggies will be pining.

HENRY. I'll get a contract. Give me the office key, Philip.

PHILIP. Philips.

HENRY. Whatever your damn name is! Give me the key to the office.

JOANNA. No! (Moving to desk.) Save time, use some of our notepaper.

(She takes a sheet from the drawer and a pen. She hands the paper to HENRY and the pen to MISS SMYTHE. HENRY takes out his own pen and writes out a brief contract.)

MISS SMYTHE (to ALISTAIR). I'm sure we can keep it straightforward and simple, Mr. Markham. (ALISTAIR is lost in his own thoughts.) Mr. Markham!

(ALISTAIR is still "miles away" so PHILIP slaps the back of his head. ALISTAIR "comes to" and PHILIP quickly turns the slap into "hair tidying" for MISS SMYTHE's benefit.)

ALISTAIR. I'm sorry. I was miles away.

MISS SMYTHE. Oh, were you? I would have thought this transaction was of some interest to you.

HENRY. Indeed it is.

JOANNA. Indeed it is.

PHILIP. Indeed it is, madam. I daresay the master was ruminating on the question of commission, which will be at the usual rate. And length of agreement, which I suggest will be initially for three years.

(He gets his head between HENRY and MISS SMYTHE scrutinising what HENRY is writing.)

MISS SMYTHE (to JOANNA). He's got rather a lot to say for a butler.

HENRY (still writing). You and I can initial this now, Miss Smythe, and draw up a formal one as soon as possible.

MISS SMYTHE. Yes, well, my only concern as I was saying to Mrs. Markham (sees PHILIP's head in the way) are you quite sure you can hear? As I was saying to Mrs. Markham, my only concern is that your firm does not get involved with immorality and sex.

PHILIP. The times I've said that to Mr. Markham.

MISS SMYTHE (looking at her fingers). Oh dear, leaky pen. (She rises.) May I use your bathroom?

JOANNA. Yes.

PHILIP. Yes.

HENRY. No!

PHILIP. No!

MISS SMYTHE (startled, she sits). Oh.

PHILIP (hastily). We've just had the decorator in there, and it's in a ghastly mess.

ALISTAIR (piqued). It's looking simply divine, I don't know—

HENRY (quickly). Down, boy, down!

JOANNA. Henry, for heaven's sake.

(During her ensuing speech PHILIP hastily whispers in her ear that there is a naked girl in the bathroom.)

JOANNA (cont.). If Miss Smythe wants to wash her hands there is no possible reason why she shouldn't use the bathroom, which is looking absolutely gorgeous and if she is—STARK!

MISS SMYTHE. What?

PHILIP. The decor's rather stark.

MISS SMYTHE (rising). That won't worry me, I assure you.

(MISS SMYTHE takes a step towards the bedroom door, HENRY nips in in front of her.)

HENRY. First come, first served.

(He dives through the bedroom door, slams it, and goes into the dressing room at top speed.)

MISS SMYTHE. Well, really. But what about my inky pinkies?

PHILIP. Perhaps madam would care to use the hand basin in the study.

(Opens study door.)

MISS SMYTHE. Yes, I suppose so, but that doesn't excuse Mr. Lodge's behaviour.

PHILIP. You must forgive him. It's an old war wound.

(They exit into study.)

ALISTAIR. What was that all about?

JOANNA. I'm not quite sure, but I think Philip's got a naked girl in the bathroom.

ALISTAIR (laughs with delight). Oo! Packs a lot into a day, doesn't he.

(LINDA rushes in from the front door.)

LINDA. Darling—darling! Disaster.

JOANNA. What is it?

LINDA. That office is nothing but interruptions. First the door rattled, then the phone buzzed. Poor Walter's such a bag of nerves, he can't do a thing with me.

ALISTAIR. Try him with a cup of tea, dear.

LINDA. It's put him right off.

JOANNA. Let me put you both off. It was Henry.

LINDA. Henry?

ALISTAIR. It's alright, he's out on parole.

LINDA. Parole?

JOANNA. From Bow Street, but that's not important. He's involved with Miss Smythe.

LINDA. Miss Smythe, who's she?

JOANNA. Never mind, but you can't meet her.

LINDA. Why can't I meet her?

JOANNA. Because Philip's the butler, Alistair's Philip and we've got a dog in the basket. So don't put your foot in it.

LINDA. I haven't understood a word of that.

ALISTAIR. You forgot to mention the naked girl in the bathroom.

JOANNA. Yes!

LINDA. But where's Henry?

ALISTAIR. In the bathroom.

LINDA. This time he's gone too far.

(She strides into the bedroom followed by JOANNA and ALISTAIR, who closes the door.)

JOANNA. Linda, from what I gather Philip's after her.

LINDA (surprised). Philip?

ALISTAIR. Yes. He might stop pestering your Henry now.

(During the ensuing dialogue WALTER creeps in whispering quietly—"Lindy-loo". Hears the voices in the bedroom, but as he goes towards it, the study door opens and PHILIP and MISS SMYTHE are heard talking. WALTER very quickly dashes into the bar and closes the door.)

JOANNA. Alistair, you could be sued for some of the things you've said here this evening. (To LINDA.) All you need to know is that Miss Smythe is in the study. Now clear off.

PHILIP (off). After you, madam.

MISS SMYTHE (entering). Thank you very much.

(MISS SMYTHE and PHILIP enter from study at the same time as JOANNA pushes in LINDA followed by ALISTAIR. They come face to face and stop.)

JOANNA (loudly and clearly to LINDA). This is Miss Smythe—the famous authoress—who is now in the process of being signed up by Mr. Markham (points to ALISTAIR) and Mr. Lodge. (Points to the bedroom.) And Alistair is the dog.

LINDA. Huh?

ALISTAIR (flatly). Woof, woof.

(LINDA and MISS SMYTHE look baffled.)

PHILIP (even louder). And I'm the butler.

MISS SMYTHE (deafened). Is it necessary to shout?

PHILIP. Yes! If I may be so bold.

JOANNA (to LINDA). You savvy now?

LINDA. Er—

PHILIP. You go now. You no come back. (To MISS SMYTHE.) She foreign.

MISS SMYTHE. Me understand.

(LINDA is about to speak.)

JOANNA (to MISS SMYTHE). She Miss Hauser. (To ALISTAIR.) Sylvie—late—back—Philip.

ALISTAIR. You—naughty—girl—Sylvie.

LINDA. Sylvie?

PHILIP. Ah, English improving. Very good, missy.

JOANNA (to MISS SMYTHE). Sylvie is our girl.

MISS SMYTHE. I thought I'd already met your girl.

JOANNA. Did you?

MISS SMYTHE. Yes. Long in the leg and short in the nightie.

JOANNA. Ah, yes. That's our *other* girl. Helga.

LINDA. Helga?

JOANNA. Yes. Helga. Your sister.

LINDA. Sister?

JOANNA. Yes—You can go now, Sylvie.

LINDA. Where?

JOANNA. To Helga!

(PHILIP pulls LINDA to one side.)

PHILIP. Sylvie. While master—(points to ALISTAIR) have pow-wow about heap-big writer (points to MISS SMYTHE) you go make big heap sandwiches.

LINDA (after some deliberation). Ja.

JOANNA. Lovely. Yes. We all starving. What would you like, Miss Smythe? Cheese, tomato?

ALISTAIR. Sauerkraut, pumpernickel?

MISS SMYTHE. Anything simple. Pheasant, if you have it.

PHILIP (pointedly). The speciality of the house is goose!

MISS SMYTHE (after some consideration). I haven't had that lately.

(The others look up to heaven.)

JOANNA (to LINDA). Thank you, Sylvie.

LINDA (approaching MISS SMYTHE). Auf wiedersehen—

JOANNA (pushing LINDA to hallway). On second thoughts, I'll come with you and explain what is required of you!

LINDA (enjoying herself). Oh-ja! Ve vill to ze kitchen-*hauser*-gegoen*hauser*—for ze gesandwichen*hauser*—howzat?

JOANNA. Louser, Miss Hauser!

(JOANNA pushes her off and they both exit to kitchen.)

MISS SMYTHE. Mr. Markham. I think this delayed honeymoon is affecting your wife.

ALISTAIR. Shall we call it a postponement?

PHILIP. We'll call it a cancellation.

MISS SMYTHE (tersely). Philips. (To ALISTAIR.) Where are you going for your honeymoon?

ALISTAIR. We thought we'd have it at home. (Grins at PHILIP.)

MISS SMYTHE. What on earth would you find to do there all day?

ALISTAIR. You'd be surprised!

(PHILIP reacts to this.)

MISS SMYTHE. You should try the Norfolk Broads. You could visit my beautiful grounds. They're a picture. This latest man of mine has a wonderful way with flora. And it's so peaceful. That's why I bury them all in the garden. The dogs, that is, not the gardener.

PHILIP. Well I went on the Broads once and got terrible bronchitis.

(HENRY backs on from the dressing room, followed by a remonstrating MISS WILKINSON. The following dialogue in each room is spoken simultaneously but MISS WILKINSON's is predominant.)

MISS S. I refuse to believe that.

PHILIP. It's an absolute fact. I've never been the same since.

MISS S. But they're an important part of our national heritage. Don't you agree, Mr. Markham?

ALISTAIR. Absolutely.

HENRY. For goodness sake be reasonable.

MISS W. I want my clothes.

HENRY. Shh!

MISS W. And I want to go home.

HENRY. Alright, alright.

MISS W. It's no fun standing in nothing but a sheet.

HENRY. I've said I'll get your clothes.

MISS W. And be jolly quick about it.

(By this time HENRY has pushed MISS WILKINSON off into the dressing room and is returning to the living room door.)

MISS SMYTHE. I can't accept that Norfolk anything to do with your bronchitis, Philips. Everybody finds them very beneficial.

(HENRY enters, locks the door and puts the key in his jacket pocket.)

MISS SMYTHE (cont.). Ah, Mr. Lodge, what do you know about the Broads?

HENRY (instantly guilty). Never touched her! Never touched her!

MISS SMYTHE. Eh?—What?

PHILIP. If I may be so bold sir, madam was referring to the geographical variety on the East Coast.

HENRY. Oh I see.

MISS SMYTHE. Philips was saying that he suffered from some congestion in the Norfolk area.

HENRY. He's got a similar problem in the Bath area.

MISS SMYTHE. Dear me. (To PHILIP.) It might be safer if you stayed at home in future.

PHILIP (glancing at ALISTAIR). I have every intention of doing so.

MISS SMYTHE (looks at her watch). And I must get to mine too. Where are those few notes you jotted down, Mr. Lodge?

HENRY. Here we are Miss Smythe.

(He picks it up from the table and hands it to her.)

MISS SMYTHE. Thank you. I'm so looking forward to our association.

(As she reads it, HENRY pulls PHILIP to one side.)

HENRY. Miss Wilkinson is getting difficult. What the hell have you done with her drawers?
PHILIP (whispers). In the bar.
ALISTAIR. No whispering, Philips! If you've anything worth saying, say it out loud.
PHILIP. Quite so. I was merely saying that such an auspicious occasion calls for a celebratory drink.
MISS SMYTHE. Splendid, I never got my sherry.
PHILIP. I think champagne would be appropriate.
MISS SMYTHE. Delicious. Just a sip.
PHILIP. Then if you'll excuse me I'll crack a bottle.

(He does his stiff butler's walk to the bar.)

ALISTAIR. Walk like that and you'll crack something.

(PHILIP stops, glowers at him and then continues to the bar. He opens it and comes face to face with WALTER who steps out nervously with a fatuous grin and holding a glass.)

WALTER (to PHILIP). Hullo-ee. (To ALISTAIR.) Hulo-ee. (To MISS SMYTHE.) Hullo-ee. (To HENRY.) My card.
HENRY. You're new around here, aren't you?

(JOANNA enters from the hall.)

JOANNA. Your pumpernickel and sauerkraut sandwich won't be a—(sees WALTER). Ahh! Where did you come from?
MISS SMYTHE (points casually to the dispensary). Usual place.
JOANNA (to WALTER). Have you introduced yourself to anyone?
WALTER. Er—no.

JOANNA. Good, then I can do it. Miss Smythe.

WALTER. Good evening.

JOANNA. Philips, the butler.

WALTER. Good evening.

JOANNA. And Mr. Henry Lodge.

WALTER. Good night. (He takes his card back quickly.)

PHILIP. Perhaps madam would care to tell us who this is, if she'd be so bold.

JOANNA. Certainly.

PHILIP (angrily). I suppose he's another of your—

JOANNA (quickly). No, no. He's my father-in-law.

(Everyone digests this piece of news, then turns to look back at ALISTAIR.)

ALISTAIR (after a pause). Hullo, Daddy.

WALTER. Yes—er—Alistair.

PHILIP. He's in the basket, sir.

WALTER. Basket?

HENRY. Basket.

MISS SMYTHE (bemused). How long have you been in there, Mr.—er—

WALTER (quickly). Pangbourne.

ALISTAIR (quickly). Spenlow!

JOANNA (quickly). Markham!!

WALTER. Markham. (Then looks at ALISTAIR.) Markham?

JOANNA. He's been in there ever since the wedding reception. He got tiddly.

WALTER. What wedding?

JOANNA. And he's still tiddly. (To WALTER.) Can't you remember, father-in-law? My wedding to Philip. (Points to ALISTAIR.)

WALTER. Oh, ah, yes, that wedding.

MISS SMYTHE (to WALTER). If your son takes as long over his honeymoon as he has over this contract, your wife will never be a grandmother.

WALTER. I'll convey your message. I think I'll be going now.

ALISTAIR. That's right. Mummy will be worried about you.

WALTER. Toodle-pip.

MISS SMYTHE. I say, Mr. Markham.

PHILIP
WALTER ⎱ (all turn together). Yes?
ALISTAIR ⎰

MISS SMYTHE (to PHILIP). Philips stop sticking your oar in, (to ALISTAIR.) Anyway, I was referring to your father, Mr. Markham.

ALISTAIR. That's you Daddy.

WALTER. Oh. (To MISS SMYTHE.) Yes?

MISS SMYTHE (referring to his glass). I should leave that if I were you. They're getting rather low on glasses.

WALTER. Oh yes.

(He moves back into the bar as LINDA enters with a little apron on and carrying a tray with the sandwiches.)

LINDA. Damen und Herren. Ich bin hir mit ze sandwichen.

(She finds herself standing next to HENRY, who looks baffled. She smiles at him confidently and then turns to MISS SMYTHE and speaks in broken English as WALTER emerges.)

LINDA (cont.). Here is the most lovely—(sees WALTER) *pumpernickel*!!

(The tray flies into the air and then everybody joins in collecting the sandwiches together.)

JOANNA (eventually) (points to LINDA and WALTER.) Oh, you two haven't met. (To MISS SMYTHE.) Sylvie's very nervous when she sees a new face. (Loudly to SYLVIE.) Don't—be—shy—Sylvie.

MISS SMYTHE (holding her ear). We'll all be deaf in a minute.

LINDA. I only shy when strange men I am seeing.

HENRY. What are you talking like that for?

LINDA. Like vot for?

HENRY. You're not Irish are you?

JOANNA. This is Sylvie, the maid from the Continent.

HENRY. Sylvie, the maid?

ALISTAIR. And this is Walter.

PHILIP. The father-in-law from the cupboard.

LINDA. Father-in-law? Vas is das

JOANNA (points to WALTER). I'll tell you vas das is. Das is (points to ALISTAIR) his father, and he is appearing very suddenly.

LINDA. And going very quickerly!

HENRY. Could we have a re-cap?

PHILIP. Good idea, Mr. Lodge, let's start from the father-in-law.

HENRY. Let's start from that damn dog . . .

MISS SMYTHE. Let's start from our agreement or I'm going home.

PHILIP ⎱ (together). One moment madam.
HENRY ⎰ No, please.

LINDA (Picking up sandwiches). I will brush down the sandwiches, Fraulein Schmidt.

MISS SMYTHE. No, they'll do as they are. A bit of fluff never harmed anyone, did it, Mr. Lodge?

HENRY. No. Indeed.

MISS SMYTHE (bending over and looks at her sandwich). I haven't been given the speciality of the house.

PHILIP. Stick around, madam.

(PHILIP, without thinking, gives her a quick backward version of the goose.)

MISS SMYTHE. Ahhh!!

(MISS SMYTHE is aghast. So is everybody else, including PHILIP who is bowing, and apologising in dumb show.)

PHILIP. I do apologise.

MISS SMYTHE. What on earth happened to me?

PHILIP. I regret to say you were the recipient of a—(he mimes the backward goose and whistles.)

MISS SMYTHE. Good heavens.

HENRY. I can assure you, Miss Smythe, it's far less serious than a—(he mimes the forward goose and whistles.)

ALISTAIR. Unless you're one of the Portsmouth broads.

MISS SMYTHE. What came over you, Philips?

PHILIP. I'm abjectly sorry, madam. I did it on an impulse.

MISS SMYTHE. I know what you did it on.

JOANNA. It won't happen again. Do sit down.

MISS SMYTHE. I think I'd better.

(She sits down slowly eyeing the men warily in case she gets another "goose".)

MISS SMYTHE (cont.). Now where was I with the contract?

LINDA (to ALISTAIR). I will be in ze kitchen, if you desire me, Mr. Markham.

ALISTAIR. I'll remember that, Syvlie.

LINDA (bowing to everyone). Gutte nacht, Frau Markham, Gutte nacht, mein butler, gutte nacht, Vater-in-law, gutte nacht, Fraulein Schmidt und gutte nacht, Herr Stodge.

HENRY. Lodge. I suppose *you* know what you're doing?

LINDA. Ja. I am to the kitchen going. Is there something I can take with me?

JOANNA (looking at WALTER). Oh mein Papa.

LINDA. Oh ja, kommen zie hier und please to help me wiz ze up-washing.

WALTER. Yes of course. Up washing?

(He goes into the hallway.)

JOANNA. Thank you, Sylvie.

LINDA. Auf wiedersehen, everybody.

(She bows standing next to ALISTAIR.)

ALISTAIR (without thinking). So long, Sylvie.

(He gooses her. LINDA gives a scream and exits.)

HENRY. What the blazes—

MISS SMYTHE. What's the matter with your girl?

ALISTAIR. Yodel practice.

MISS SMYTHE. Could we just return to this agreement and forget the yodelling, the unfortunately delayed honeymoon and the unexpected arrival of your father-in-law.

HENRY. Certainly, at once. Is everything to your complete satisfaction?

MISS SMYTHE. Yes, everything.

HENRY. Marvellous.

JOANNA. Wonderful.

PHILIP. Super-doops. I can't tell you how happy . . .

MISS SMYTHE. Oh my God, he's off again.

(MISS SMYTHE glowers at PHILIP for his latest interruption. PHILIP bows and backs up to the bedroom door.)

HENRY. Are you sure you're completely satisfied.

MISS SMYTHE. Yes, everything except for this three year option.

(MISS WILKINSON enters from the dressing room, still wrapped in her sheet, and during the following dialogue goes to the living room door and tries to open it. PHILIP hears the handle turn and furtively gets to the door.)

HENRY. Make it seven then.

MISS SMYTHE. No, no, twelve months is what I had in mind.

HENRY. Is that all?

MISS SMYTHE. Initially. Just while we get to know each other.

HENRY. Well I don't know whether twelve months is long enough really.

(MISS WILKINSON decides not to get kept waiting and bangs on door three times. ALISTAIR, JOANNA and HENRY freeze. MISS SMYTHE turns enquiringly to PHILIP's direction. He smiles and bangs his foot three times.)

MISS SMYTHE. Mrs. Markham, does your butler have to be here?

JOANNA. Yes, I think he does.

MISS SMYTHE (to ALISTAIR). Have you checked his references, Mr. Markham?

ALISTAIR. Oh. Yes.

MISS SMYTHE. Where on earth did you get him from?

ALISTAIR (to JOANNA). Where did we get him from?

JOANNA. Universal Aunts.

MISS SMYTHE. Well could we please get on without any further interruptions.

HENRY. I hope so.

(MISS WILKINSON bangs rapidly on the door and everyone looks at PHILIP who obliges with a quick demonstration of flamenco foot tapping.)

PHILIP. Olé.

MISS SMYTHE. You say you got him from Universal Aunts.

JOANNA. Highly recommended.

MISS SMYTHE. I should send him back if I were you.

HENRY. I'll alter this then to twelve months, Miss Smythe, and you and I can initial each clause.

(PHILIP hurries into bar and immediately gets MISS WILKINSON's dress, bra and pants. He goes to the bedroom door but finds it locked.)

MISS SMYTHE. Yes, I think I'm agreeable.
HENRY. Splendid. Here we are then.

(He initials the first clause and passes the sheet of paper to MISS SMYTHE.)

PHILIP (whispering hoarsely through the louvres of the door). Hang on, I'll get the key.

(He drops clothes by bedroom door and goes quickly to HENRY.)

HENRY. That's it. Now I'll do the second one. Now you. (PHILIP tugs his arm.) Buzz off. (PHILIP tugs again.) Buzz off.

MISS SMYTHE (PHILIP tugs again). Buzz off—! If I may be so bold.

HENRY (referring to contract). That's the one. Now you.

(While MISS SMYTHE signs her second clause, PHILIP tugs again at HENRY's sleeve. HENRY mimes for him to get back to the door. While HENRY tries to initial the next clause PHILIP slips his hand into HENRY's trouser pocket, frantically feeling for the key. This contorts HENRY and makes it extremely difficult for him to sign. At the same time he is preventing MISS SMYTHE from seeing his contortions.)

MISS SMYTHE. There we are then.
HENRY. And finally, Miss Smythe, our last initials go here.
MISS SMYTHE. Yes, yes I think that completes it.

(Noticing the last of HENRY's contortions.) The old war wound playing you up again?

      (PHILIP has given up searching for the key and darts up to the bedroom door.)

PHILIP (whispering through the door). Stand by.

      (He feeds the dress and the pants into the louvres, which MISS WILKINSON pulls through.)

MISS SMYTHE. Oh, one more thing. Mr. Lodge, our initials will require witnessing.
JOANNA. May I?
MISS SMYTHE. An independent witness, Mrs. Markham. (Calls to PHILIP.) Philips?

      (PHILIP stops and turns in the act of pushing the bra through the louvres. MISS WILKINSON has hold of one strap. The other strap is looped over PHILIP's wrist. MISS WILKINSON keeps tugging which results in PHILIP's hand banging the door at regular intervals. MISS WILKINSON finally gives a strong tug pulling the bra through, at the same time rapping PHILIP's knuckles. PHILIP who has nearly lost a hand through the door, is jumping up and down, shaking his hand in agony. MISS WILKINSON has exited quickly to dressing room.)

MISS SMYTHE (cont.). *Now* what's he up to?
HENRY. Damn vicious, these labradoodles.
MISS SMYTHE (rising). Oh do let me see your Alistair.

      (PHILIP, HENRY and JOANNA all restrain her, and PHILIP hastily initials the agreement.)

JOANNA. No no, he'll have gone back to his basket exhausted.
HENRY. Besides, you'll miss your train.
MISS SMYTHE. Oh dear me, that would never do. Now let me make sure that I've got my ticket.
JOANNA. Can I help you.

(As she fumbles in her handbag HENRY pulls PHILIP aside.)

HENRY. Have you gone raving mad?
PHILIP. I wanted the key.
HENRY. Well, why didn't you ask for it?

(He takes it out of his jacket pocket and unlocks the bedroom door.)

MISS SMYTHE (finding ticket). Here it is. It's such a relief to be with a healthy upright team.
HENRY. We'll send you a proper contract before the end of the week.
MISS SMYTHE. Thank you.

(SYLVIE enters purposefully from the hallway in a raincoat with a headscarf, having plucked up courage to speak her mind.)

SYLVIE. I'm very sorry, Mrs. Markham, but I have come to tell you that I have given the matter a lot of thinking. I cannot stay here any longer with the cuddlings, the keyholes and the goosings.

(MISS SMYTHE looks round for some sort explanation, but doesn't get one.)

SYLVIE (cont.). And it's no use anyone trying to change my mind. All I want is for Alistair to carry my cases downstairs.
MISS SMYTHE (after a slight pause). He's not quite up to that, is he?
JOANNA. Wait till his nose is cold.
SYLVIE (ignoring this—to ALISTAIR). I shall be in my room. (Then turns to PHILIP.) I want you to know that I have been very very happy with you but I hope you understand why I must go. Goodbye, and thank you for everything.

(She exits quickly. Everyone looks non-plussed.)

MISS SMYTHE. Excuse me. What was all that about?

(Everyone stands rigid with their thoughts racing.)

PHILIP. God. My wife's leaving me.

(He sinks dramatically into a chair. Everybody takes in what he has said. JOANNA and HENRY look pleased and MISS SMYTHE very concerned as MISS WILKINSON storms out of the bedroom in her bra and pants, putting on her dress. She goes through the lounge and out into the hall. MISS SMYTHE looks dumbfounded.)

MISS SMYTHE. And that is er—
HENRY. Why his wife's leaving him.
MISS SMYTHE (to PHILIP). Well I hope you've learnt something from all this.
PHILIP. My God, I have.
MISS SMYTHE. I'll bid you all good night.
PHILIP. I'll see you out, Madam.
MISS SMYTHE. I'd like to say I've enjoyed my visit this evening.
JOANNA. Thank you.
MISS SMYTHE (pointedly to PHILIP). Yes, I'd *like* to say that.

(She exits followed by PHILIP ushering her out.)

HENRY. Well, we pulled it off. By George it's magnificent. Well done, Jo. (Embraces her and kisses her.) And you too, Alistair.

(He goes towards ALISTAIR who scuttles away from HENRY, thinking that he too might get a kiss.)

ALISTAIR. Don't you dare.
HENRY. I don't know how we managed it, but she'll be the biggest money spinner we've ever had.

(PHILIP returns.)

HENRY (cont.). Congratulations, partner.
PHILIP (bearing down on JOANNA). Alright now, who was that man in the cupboard.
JOANNA (standing her ground). Nothing to do with me.
PHILIP. Oh no, just in there reading the meter, I suppose.

JOANNA. Who was that girl who blew out of the bedroom?
PHILIP. Nothing to do with me.
JOANNA. Just taking a short cut to Selfridges, I suppose.
HENRY. Matter of fact, old love, she's G.P.O.
JOANNA. Yes—Good Push Over.
PHILIP ⎫ (together). You can talk, you've had two lovers
⎬   here.
HENRY ⎭ She was just cleaning the phone actually—

(LINDA enters in the middle of the previous speech.)

LINDA. Joanna darling, I think we'd better—

(Everybody now speaks at once.)

PHILIP (together). I've been faithful for fifteen years, fifteen long years and the only bit of relaxation I've had is a round of golf—
HENRY (together). Now look here, Linda, I feel I'm entitled to know why you were talking double dutch and passing yourself off as Sylvie—
JOANNA (together). When I think of all the things you've called me tonight, you're damn lucky I haven't packed my bags and gone—
LINDA (together). Don't you talk to me, Henry Lodge, I've put up with your affairs for years and you'd be a lot safer in Bow Street—

(While they are all talking ALISTAIR collects his clothing from the bedroom. He then returns and silences them with a piercing whistle.)

ALISTAIR. If you're all going to have a row, I'm going to have a couple of Bob Martins.

(ALISTAIR exits hallway.)

PHILIP (to JOANNA). Let's have it now, who was Walter, the father-in-law?
LINDA. None of this has anything to do with you Philip.
PHILIP. Oh no, Mr. Spenlow's banging away in the bedroom while Walter's waiting to be called on as substitute.
JOANNA. Will you listen?

PHILIP. God, I'll kill him.

HENRY. Simmer down, old man. Simmer down.

(He pats PHILIP consolingly on both shoulders.)

PHILIP. It's alright for you.

HENRY (pats him again). Must be a hell of a shock, I know, but blowing your top won't help. Come on, Jo, let's have the truth.

LINDA. It's got nothing to do with her either.

HENRY. Hasn't it?

LINDA. Walter's all mine.

HENRY. There you are, Philip, it had nothing to do with eith— He is what!? D'you mean to say you've been having an affair?

LINDA. I've been doing my best under very trying circumstances.

HENRY. God, I'll kill him!

PHILIP (enjoying himself as he pats HENRY). Simmer down, old man, simmer down.

HENRY. It's alright for you.

PHILIP (pats him again). Must be a hell of a—

HENRY. Shut up! (Then to LINDA.) D'you mean to say you find this fellow more attractive than me?

LINDA. No, just more available.

HENRY. Right, from now on I'm home every night.

JOANNA (to LINDA). Well done, darling. Bugs Bunny rides again.

HENRY. Come on you.

LINDA. Where?

HENRY. Home.

LINDA. First stop the bedroom?

HENRY. No first stop the kitchen.

LINDA. What for?

HENRY. To put that bloody kettle on.

(They exit into hall. PHILIP and JOANNA look at each other for a moment.)

PHILIP. My Jo-Jo. (He goes to embrace her.)

JOANNA. Wait a minute—that G.P.O. girl. Is she the one who was naked?

PHILIP. Yes.

JOANNA. And she came here to strip for Henry?

PHILIP. Well, she came for Henry—but she stripped for me.

JOANNA (amazed). Philip.

PHILIP (with bravura). Yes and I was absolutely—

JOANNA. What?

PHILIP. Terrified.

(JOANNA laughs and kisses him. ALISTAIR enters with SYLVIE from U.R. of hallway.)

SYLVIE. Please don't wait up for us.

ALISTAIR. Sylvie's taking Alistair for walkies.

(SYLVIE and ALISTAIR exit L. of hallway.)

PHILIP. Tell you one thing, I've been working far too hard for years.

JOANNA. That's what I've always said.

PHILIP. You have. So, starting from now, you and I are going to have the most wonderful two weeks holiday.

JOANNA. Fabulous. Where are we going to spend it?

PHILIP. In bed.

(He picks her up and they move across the room, embracing, to the bedroom door. MISS SMYTHE enters from the hallway and picks up her briefcase which she has left behind on the sofa. She is then rooted to the spot on seeing the "butler" kissing MRS. MARKHAM in the doorway. She is even more flabbergasted when PHILIP carries JOANNA through into the bedroom and lays her on the bed. MISS SMYTHE edges her way to peep through the door. PHILIP kisses JOANNA swiftly up one arm, across her neck and is halfway down the other arm when his eyes meet MISS SMYTHE's. He stops frozen. JOANNA takes in the situation and smiles graciously at MISS SMYTHE.)

JOANNA (then to PHILIP.) That'll be all for tonight, thank you, Philips.

PHILIP (bows). Very good, madam.

(PHILIP walks to the door indicating to MISS SMYTHE that she should leave. An astonished MISS SMYTHE starts to walk out as the CURTAIN FALLS.)

PROPERTY PLOT

ACT 1

ON STAGE

Pen on dressing table
Telephone on dressing table.
Intercom telephone with buzzer
and ordinary telephone on small
desk.
Drinks etc. in drink cupbaord.
Alistair's pinking shears.
Sheet of writing paper in
between sofa cushions.
Deodorant on window sill for
Joanna.
Tape measure on desk for
Alistair.
Joanna puts her handbag on
desk.

OFF STAGE

Parcels and handbag—Joanna.
Hat and gloves—Joanna.
Curtain material and tape
measure—Alistair.
Handbag in which there is a
three-page letter—Linda.
Several children's books—Philip.
Slim briefcase containing
pyjama tops—Henry.
Curtains and chair covers—Alistair.
Black dress—Joanna.
Cup fo coffee on tray—Sylvie.
Watch—Henry.
Dress and pair of shoes—Joanna.
Two gaudy cushions—Alistair.
Towelled dressing gown and
attractive shower hat—Joanna.
Bottle of champagne—Linda.
Torn and oily strip of the letter—
Philip.
Two gaudy cushions—
Alistair.
Watch—Joanna.
Catalogues and samples—Alistair.
Henry—pipe.
Shoulder bag—Sylvie.

PROPERTY PLOT—*cont.*

ACT 2

ON STAGE

Counterpane on bed.
Watch—Alistair.
Pencil and notepad on desk L. to
R. Telephone Directory.
Champagne and two glasses.
Sheet of notepaper from the
desk drawer.

OFF STAGE

Scarlet nightie—Joanna.
Pyjamas in bedroom—Alistair.
Champagne, roses, umbrella and
the note on desk—Walter.
Shoulder bag containing
shortie-nightie.
Tray with champagne and two
glasses—Joanna.
Visiting cards—Walter.
Vanity case—Linda.
Briefcase and handbag, and
manuscript in briefcase—
Miss Smythe.
Watch—Miss Smythe.
Raffle tickets—Henry.
Tea towel tucked into his
trousers—Philip.
Pen—Henry.
Tray of sandwiches and wearing
a little apron—Linda.
Miss Wilkinson wrapped in sheet.
Key—Henry.

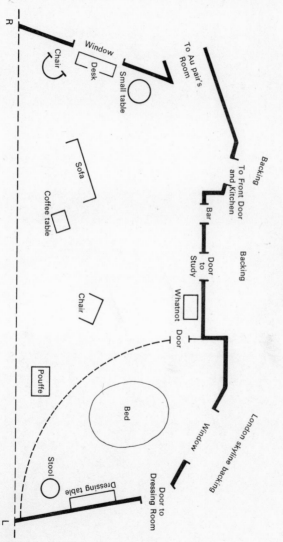

STAGE PLAN

15/104